SCUOLA GRANDE DEI CARMINI

UMBERTO FRANZOI
FRANCA LUGATO

Vianello
LIBRI

Scuola Grande dei Carmini

history and architecture
Umberto Franzoi

art
Franca Lugato

editorial design
Scibilia & Scibilia

archive research
Martina Massaro

editor
Andrea Montagnani

editorial assistants
Alba Borella
Bernardo Apolli
Federica Centulani

english translation
Giles Watson

photographic references
Cameraphoto Arte, Venice
Archivio Museo Correr, Venice

© 2003 edizioni Grafiche Vianello srl / Vianello Libri
Ponzano (Treviso) Italy
info@vianellolibri.com
www.vianellolibri.com

isbn 88-7200-138-2

cover illustration
10 Giambattista Tiepolo,
*The Virgin Bestowing the Scapular
on Saint Simon Stock,*
(detail) oil on canvas, 533 x 432 cm.

page 2
17 Giambattista Tiepolo,
Fortitude and Justice
(detail) oil on canvas, 235 x 240 cm.

Scuola Grande dei Carmini

Contents

The Scuole – Venice's Schools of Devotion and Schools of Arts and Crafts

"Scuola", from the Greek *scholè*, then Latin *schola*, originally meant "rest and free use of one's own spiritual forces", or an institution whose purpose is education and instruction. By analogy, the term was applied to organisations set up to teach various spiritual or craft techniques.

The Scuola (plural Scuole) was thus a place where people met to learn, teach and talk, but also to protect the interests of their social class, intellectual pursuit or craft.

The general, almost abstract, concept of Scuola later came to have different connotations as society it self evolved.

The most interesting aspect of Venice's Scuole is their role as Associations or Confraternities of lay citizens who, in order to pursue specific aims, placed themselves under the patronage of religious figures, such as Christ, the Virgin or a saint.

These were the Scuole di Penitenza o di Devozione (Schools of Penitence or of Devotion), founded for the purpose of teaching and practising the Christian virtues, and for charitable initiatives in favour of poor, underprivileged, sick or infirm Brethren. Assistance could be either spiritual or take a more practical form, in the distribution of food and clothing, the assignment of a lodging *per amore Dei* ("for the love of God", in other words without charge), or the provision of a dowry for deserving young women to enable them to marry or enter a convent.

At Venice, the devotional Scuole were some of the wealthiest, and most important, of the charitable Confraternities. Important factors were their specialist nature, their unflagging commitment, the personal

18 Giambattista Tiepolo,
Patience, Innocence and Chastity
detail, 1743
oil on canvas, 235 x 240 cm.

generosity and selflessness of the better-off Brethren, their excellent organisation and, in most cases, the probity with which they were managed.

Members, known as Confratelli, or Brothers, were strictly non-clerical and belonged to the sector of society that until recently might have been called middle class, in the sense of non-noble. These were the so-called "original citizens", born and resident in Venice, who had been active in the crafts and professions for more than fifteen years, and were in many cases very wealthy.

The Scuola was a lay organisation, notwithstanding the prominent and very intense religious dimension that derived from rigorously observed daily devotions and close links with both a parish and a monastery church. This secular nature was frequently emphasised both by the institution itself and above all by the Republic of Venice, which stressed the point in two decrees issued in 1475 and 1498. Priests were allowed to enrol from time to time, but always with an implicit exclusion from any executive position. The clergy were, however, free to exercise a role of spiritual support and assistance. Generally, the chaplain was chosen from the priests and friars of the church or monastery connected to the Scuola. The individuals who met at these devotional or professional associations were, more or less consciously, seeking for themselves and their families some form of protection against life's imponderables. They were seeking hope to offset future – and in many cases all too present – adversities. The help that other members could provide for a colleague in difficulty meant that Brothers felt psychologically protected, both during their lifetimes and beyond, for the Scuola also prayed and interceded for the dead.

The success of the Scuole derived largely from this hope of material assistance and spiritual salvation.

All the Brothers could contribute, taking the initiative in their own lives and in those of others. The Confraternities reduced members' uncertainties about the future, their apprehensions about destitution, illness and loneliness, and lessened their dread of death and divine retribution for their sins.

It is clear that the Scuole, based on the fundamental concept of mutual assistance, were extremely important for the Venetian lower middle classes.

Tasks carried out included assistance to those in prison or awaiting execution, visiting the sick and infirm, burying the dead and supporting their families.

Equally important was members' moral and religious conduct for the salvation of their own souls and those of their fellows.

Directly or indirectly, the entire Scuola system had an immense influence on social life as a whole, and on individual relations, through the honesty and mutual co-operation it demanded, and which constituted the cement that held such groups together.

This, at least in theory, was the Scuola's aim – the formation of model citizens who respected religion and the law not because they were forced to, but from a sense of personal participation in the body politic.

It is fair to say that from the Middle Ages to the fall of the Republic, Venice's Scuole and their members were responsible for a major part of the city's religious life and charitable activities. It was one way – and an effective one – to do good. The Scuole enabled large numbers of citizens to survive, thanks to the goodwill of others.

There were at Venice, as elsewhere, various kinds of Scuola.

In manufacturing and industry, guilds or corporations were known as Scuole di Arti e di Mestieri (Schools of Arts and Crafts). There were many Scuole of this kind, instituted to safeguard the interests of a category, since their membership was drawn from those who practised a specific art or craft. Through the Scuola, Brothers could obtain work and administrative assistance, for the association drew up contracts, and laid down rates and fees. Each craft was overseen by a board or council, presided by the Gastaldo, who was assisted by a Vicario.

Over time, enrolling in the Scuola became well-nigh mandatory to practise any business activity whatsoever. There were Scuole for bakers, barbers, bell ringers, boatmen, bombardiers, bricklayers, butchers, coopers, caulkers, cobblers, cabinetmakers, coppersmiths, furriers, goldsmiths, greengrocers, haberdashers, jewellers, linen merchants, painters, pastrymakers, poultry merchants, sailors, sausage makers, shopkeepers, silk merchants, squirrel furriers, stone masons, tailors, weavers, winnowers and wool merchants.

Venice also hosted many Italian and non-Italian foreign communities. These, too, gathered with the assent of the authorities in specific parts of the city, where they built their houses, church and Scuole. Such communities included the Florentines, the Milanese, the Albanians, the Greeks, the Schiavoni (Slavs), the Turks and so on.

Equally numerous were the Scuole di Devozione, whose name came from their specifically religious purpose, either of prayer or ritual devotion. Each Scuola had its own patron saint, through whom divine protection could be invoked. There were Scuole for the symbols and attributes of Christ's Passion, sacred objects like the Rosary, as well as for the Virgin, Christ, the Guardian Angel, Good Death, the Dead, the Passion, the Picai (Hanged Men), the Purification, the Holy Spirit, the Trinity, the Holy Sacrament, Saint Anthony, Saint Barbara, Saint Christopher, Saint Fantin, Saint Hyacinth, Saint Jerome, Saint John the Baptist, Saint Joseph, Saint Nicholas, Saint Pasquale Baylon, Saint Simon the Prophet, Saint Stephen, Saint Ursula and others.

The devotional Scuole brought together people from many different professions. Merchants met with contractors, lawyers, notaries, doctors, secretaries, bureaucrats from the state magistracies, wholesalers, retailers, artisans, artists, salesmen, shopkeepers, fishermen, farmers, landowners, workers, the self-employed, the salaried and finally the poor and beggars, all with a devotion to a particular saint, a willingness to help others, and all sharing the opportunity to reap the benefits that only the Scuola could provide.

It is extremely difficult to pinpoint the exact period at which the first Scuole, or Scuola-like associations, sprang up in the lagoon area. There are occasional documentary references before the year 1000 but it

Giovanni Grevembroch,
The Candle-bearer
colour drawing
(Museo Correr, Venice).

Giovanni Grevembroch,
The Flagellants
colour drawing
(Museo Correr, Venice).

was only from the mid thirteenth century that groups with shared aims – the first Scuole or confraternities – came to be formed. These were primarily devotional in nature, a direct result of the mystical, religious orientation that characterised the period.

The desire for redemption from sins, and to get nearer to God through prayer and good works, spread rapidly through all sectors of society, first in Tuscany and then in all the other regions of Italy. The movement was quick to reach the lagoon. Mortification of the flesh was a major feature of this yearning for forgiveness, both in private and at public ceremonies and events such as processions, during which participants would flay their backs, arms and legs until the blood flowed.

This extreme practice was largely undertaken by members of the Scuole, who were for this reason originally known as *Battuti* (flagellants). The first to take the name was the Scuola della Carità, and then all the others at their foundation, like the Scuola di San Teodoro, the Scuola della Misericordia, the Scuola di San Giovanni Evangelista and later also the Scuola di San Rocco, even though more than two centuries had passed since the foundation of the first Scuola.

As the desire for expiation waned, the flaying became ritual in nature, and was frequently delegated. There grew up groups of members who were paid to carry out this self-punishment. Naturally, the poorest Brethren were attracted by the fee but they were also subjected to veiled threats of being struck off the list of those eligible for charitable donations.

The Scuole di Devozione were divided into two categories, the Scuole Grandi (Great Schools) and all the others, regarded as Scuole Minori (Lesser Schools) for their more limited resources and charitable outreach.

The Scuole began to acquire the title of Grande in the mid fourteenth century, when a decision of the Council of Ten laid down that the title could be recognised only for the confraternities that had, at their foundation, the taken the name "dei Battuti o dei Disciplinati" (of the Flagellants or Disciplined). A Scuola could thus be Grande only if it was devotional, dedicated to the Christian religion, social morality, charitable works, spiritual succour and economic assistance.

According to Francesco Sansovino's detailed description of the city's districts and their traditions, published in 1581 with the title *Venezia Città Nobilissima et Singolare* (Venice the Most Noble and Singular City), there were only six Scuole Grandi: Santa Maria della Carità at Dorsoduro, founded in 1260 and the most ancient of the Scuole; San Marco at Castello, 1260–61; San Giovanni Evangelista at Santa Croce, 1261; Santa Maria in Val Verde, also known as "della Misericordia", at Cannaregio, 1261; San Rocco at San Polo, 1478; and San Teodoro at San Marco, 1550–52. Later, two others were added to the list, the Scuola della Beata Vergine del Rosario, based at the church of Santi Giovanni e Paolo at Castello, which was founded in 1575 and elevated to the rank of Scuola Grande in 1765, and the Scuola di Santa Maria del Carmelo, or "dei Carmini", at Dorsoduro, founded in 1594 and given the title "Grande" in 1767.

Each Scuola had its own written and approved regulations to observe.

Giovanni Grevembroch,
The Penitent
colour drawing
(Museo Correr, Venice).

The Mariegola of the Scuola Grande dei Carmini
Cover in embossed metal and cloth.

The collection of rules, precepts and application procedures was known originally as the Capitolare, later acquiring the definitive name of Mariegola (plural Mariegole), a variant of the Latin word *matricula*.

The Mariegole came more and more to resemble each other as all the Scuole developed along the same lines. Their text was divided into chapters that laid down the rules of the institution in matters political, religious and administrative. The Confraternity's practical and devotional aims were laid out, as were the ways in which those aims were to be pursued, and the method and timing of the election of the executive. It explained the structure of the Capitolo (Chapter) and the other governing organs, relations with the adjoining church, documentation of the Scuola's transactions and the deliberations of the Republic, and frequently also expenditure for requisites such as candles, silverware and building expenses. Also included were membership rolls, budgets and final balances, cash contributions, bequests, sums disbursed, taxes paid to the state, dowries awarded to girls of marriageable age and other details.

The supreme organ was the Capitolo, or Chapter. This assembly of Brothers elected the executive by secret ballot each year, approved the activities of the previous year and discussed plans for the future. All the Scuola's activities had to be approved by the Chapter in order to be legitimately implemented.

The highest authority, and the Scuola's most influential figure, was the Guardian Grande, corresponding to the Gastaldo in the Scuole di Arti e Mestieri. Next came the Vicario, who could act for the president in certain circumstances. Then there was the Guardian di Matin, or Morning Warden, so called because he was responsible for organising the processions, almost all of which took place before noon. The Scrivano was the chancellor, in charge of financial matters and administration, two internal auditors were elected and there was also provision for an archivist. The other members of the council, ten at most, were known as Degani or Bancali.

When almsgiving was extended to include the poor from the entire city, twelve brethren, two from each Sestiere (district) of Venice, were nominated to undertake the special task of selecting beneficiaries and distributing the alms.

In many documents, a Scuola's chancellery is referred to as the "Banca". This body would meet in the adjoining church, if the Scuola had no premises of its own, or in the Sala dell'Albergo.

In early times, the authorities placed restrictions on who could hold office in the Scuole. There were minimum age limits, viewed as a safety measure. Members elected to office had to be "original citizens", resident and working at Venice for more than twenty years, whereas the Guardian Grande had to be at least fifty years old, although the limit was reduced to forty if absolutely necessary.

The statutes of the ancient Scuole were drafted in the form of duties and rights. Above all, there was a list of actions that had to be avoided. These prohibitions ranged from blasphemy to gambling, adultery, anger, keeping bad company, frequenting prostitutes, illicit enrichment and many others, including bearing arms.

However, the list of actions that had to be performed to remit one's own and other people's sins was much longer and more demanding. First of all, Brothers had to comport themselves in word and deed in such a way as to swell the ranks of the honest. They had to perform acts of charity, give assistance to sick or infirm brethren, contribute with prayer and money to the salvation of sinful souls and hungry bodies, sustain the families of the dead during funerals and celebrate

mass for the departed. Strict observance of religious practices was enjoined, including confession, communion, fasting, abstinence, observance of feasts and hearing mass every Sunday. Finally, members had to take part in the life of the Scuola by attending, providing moral and financial support, offering donations and leaving bequests.

In short, each Brother was expected to be a model, active citizen who observed the rules of religion and of civil society. In general terms, the Republic approved of these citizens' associations and their devotional, charitable and philanthropic ends. It would not, however, allow them to operate outside the control of the state. Soon, the Venetian Scuole managed by non-patrician groups grew to acquire substantial influence in the city's economy and social structure. At that point, the government could not ignore them. Although respecting the regulations that the Scuole themselves had adopted, the Republic demanded that all such associations should be brought under government control, partly to safeguard their continued existence and partly to correct any undesirable developments. The state became the champion of the Scuole, supporting them morally and through legislation. On occasion, Venice made use of the Confraternities, demanding extraordinary financial contributions, but the state also gave Scuola representatives prominent offices, usually of a purely formal nature, during public ceremonies. The Doge, the Signoria and the Senate were happy to attend the annual festivals, but on the day prescribed by law, they audited income and expenses, the roll of members, the Scuola's assets and how they had been managed.

The success of the Scuole was such that in 1318, Venice issued a special decree to prevent the constitution of new associations in the city, and suspended enrolments at existing ones. It was only a temporary measure, applied to reorganise the sector and limit numbers until the Scuole were properly regulated with appropriate legal measures. The state wished to be informed of Scuola regulations, to approve them in advance, to intervene with periodic checks to ensure that operations were carried out in observance of regulations, and to prevent abuse.

The job of monitoring the Scuole fell to the Provveditori di Comun, a leading magistrature the special nature of whose competence made it part of many of Venice's Councils, including the Senate and the Council of Ten. In 1360, the importance of the sector was clear when all Scuola-related matters were transferred to the direct jurisdiction of the Council of Ten.

Each new Scuola was obliged to obtain the approval of this extremely powerful magistrature through the issue of an official decree at its constitution. The Scuola could have no judicial or operational existence without this authorisation which, in practice, was never denied.

Theoretically, the Republic limited the size of the Scuole, but the rule was never enforced. Often, the associations exceeded the limit without incurring sanctions. Scuole were usually authorised to enrol a maximum of six hundred members, but rarely complied with this number. Enrolments of members rich and poor frequently rose well beyond a thousand.

The Scuole Grandi were accorded a leading role in processions, especially the spectacular Corpus Domini celebrations in Piazza San Marco. Here, the Brethren in all their finery opened the parade just behind the Signoria, with the Doge, and the Patriarch and other ecclesiastical authorities. Members guilty of poor discipline bore on their shoulders *soleri*, complicated religious paintings on heavy palanquins. Over time, the Scuole Grandi acquired sufficient prestige to become a sort of social defence structure for their members, and even on occasion a means of vindication against the most powerful class. These were the only institutions where citizens and the populace of whatever social extraction, including non-Venetians, could meet, provided they maintained the original secular character in the prosecution of their Christian devotion and social charity.

Each Scuola was associated with the nearest parish or monastery church, where in return for a substantial annual contribution, it possessed an altar dedicated to its patron saint. Often, the altar was built or renovated at the expense of a Scuola Grande, or rented by a Scuola Minore, together with the space in front of the altar, where the Brothers could hear mass or attend other religious and commemorative rites.

Many if not all of the Scuole, whether devotional or professional, held their elections and administrative meetings in the church itself, or at an adjacent church building. However, when the number and income of the members was sufficiently high, the Scuola would usually purchase land on which to build its own premises. Almost without exception, these edifices where the Scuola was to carry out all its principal and ancillary activities were of great symbolic and artistic merit. Important meetings were held in the Sala Capitolare, devotional matters were attended to in the chapel on the ground floor, political and administrative business went on in the Sala dell'Albergo and accounts were kept in the Sala dell'Archivio.

The plan and functional configuration of these new buildings was established early on. The essential elements were the chapel, the council hall, the administration area, the offices, the sacristy, the treasury and the great staircase. Depending on the occasionally astonishing financial resources available, some of the Scuole became the repositories of considerable wealth. In consequence, the architecture was conceived to be imposing and monumental, clad in rich marble facings on the outside and resplendent inside with lavish painted decoration. The elaborate ceremonies held at the Scuole required that they should be adorned with splendid art collections, to paint which the leading artists of the day were summoned. The outstanding symbolic and artistic value of these works is evident in the imposing *telero* cycles by Tintoretto at San Rocco,

Giacomo Franco,
Corpus Domini Procession,
sixteenth-century engraving,
(Museo Correr, Venice).

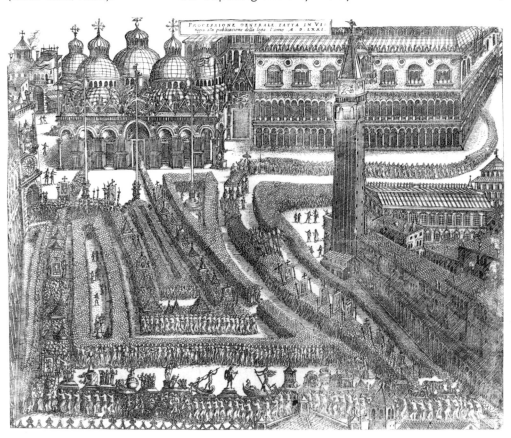

by Bellini at San Giovanni Evangelista, by Carpaccio at San Giorgio degli Schiavoni and by Tiepolo at Santa Maria dei Carmini. The core of the Scuola building was made up of two large spaces, situated one on top of the other. The ground-floor area – the Chapel – was set aside for religious ceremonies and opened directly onto the street. Above it, the Sala Capitolare was reserved for political or social functions. The staircase, often a double one, that united these two spaces was always lavishly decorated.

All this had been going on for centuries when Napoleon and his Armée d'Italie arrived in Venice.

Abruptly, the social and political context was transformed and institutions like the Scuole were swept up in the changes.

On 5 May 1806, the Scuole were abolished and their assets, including real property, were confiscated. The associations were forced to hand over all the precious objects that made up their patrimony but even then, the French were not satisfied. They completed the despoliation by ordering that the paintings in the halls and other rooms should be surrendered. Only San Rocco and the Carmini managed to save their heritage, subsequently contriving, with the other Scuole Grandi, to obtain temporary permission to hold meetings for the purpose of performing strictly religious ceremonies in the buildings, which had themselves been declared state property. All other activities, especially charitable ones, were severely prohibited. The political aim was, obviously, to break down the collective system that underpinned the Scuole.

The Scuola dei Carmini, like all the others, ceased to exist. At the same time, the legal position of the adjacent church was altered. It became a parish church after the deconsecration of the church of Santa Margherita and

Giuseppe Heintz,
Redentore Procession,
oil on canvas, seventeenth century,
(Museo Correr, Venice).

the Carmelites, like the other monastic orders, were expelled from the city.

A few decades later, some of the Scuole Grandi regained their former independent status. Again, they were governed by their assembly and managed by their chancellery, elected in accordance with their original Mariegola. It was Ferdinand I of Austria who in 1840 signed and implemented a new regulation for the Scuola dei Carmini. The new statute was, in effect, a copy of the section of the ancient Mariegola regarding the Confraternity's devotional aims. It also partially acknowledged the Scuola's freedom to elect its executive, re-instituting the Cancelleria, Guardian Grande, Vicario and Guardian di Matin.

Charitable activities, forbidden by the 1840 regulations, were permitted in 1853 by a subsequent imperial decree which gave new, if very limited, scope to what had been one of the main reasons for the creation and continued life of the Confraternity.

Times had changed. Society was evolving in increasingly different ways and the social and religious terrain on which the Scuola had thrived no longer existed.

In the new legal context, the Scuole had a new cultural function to perform, that of conserving the heritage of the past, reconfiguring their architecture and artistic treasures for the enjoyment of an increasingly large number of visitors. In effect, they became structures operating in parallel with traditional museums.

Following two pages:
The façade of the Scuola dei Carmini facing Campo di Santa Margherita. At the bottom of the calle is the side entrance of the Carmini church.

The Scuola Grande di Santa Maria del Carmelo, or Scuola dei Carmini

The Scuola dei Carmini was founded in 1594 but it was only three years later, on 18 July 1597, that it applied for official recognition by the Republic. This was granted by the Council of Ten on 22 September of the same year, thus at last allowing the Scuola's chancellery to operate in full observance of the laws laid down in mid fourteenth century.

At the time, there were already several hundred members enrolled, which made formal approval a pressing necessity. The Scuola had been recruiting, and distributing alms, for some time. It is reasonable to suppose that the organisation existed in a public form long before the last decade of the sixteenth century. There is a request dating from 1594 to the nearby monastery church, for the use of an altar for the Confraternity's ceremonies. The new institution, like its more ancient fellows, was created by lay members, in complete autonomy from religious authorities of any kind and with the same organisational structure as existing Scuole.

Why did a group of laymen, driven by the revival of religious culture in Italy, found a Scuola di Devozione at Santa Margherita in the late sixteenth century, when the situation appeared to have been stable for more than three hundred years? The reason is perhaps to be sought in the local women's religious group, which had direct links to the Carmini monastery and operated with its own distinctive structure. The organisation, also lay and devotional in nature, was for women only and had been founded long before, in the late thirteenth or early fourteenth century. It is not well documented, or easy to characterise, but it can be considered similar in some respects to the male-only Scuole. It is mentioned in the chronicles of the day by the uncomplimentary

View of the Sala Capitolare looking towards the altar of the Virgin.

name of Pinzochere dei Carmini, or "Carmini Bigots". Yet it seems to have been large, well-organised, commercially active, and run by its own executive. Given the lowly condition of women at the time, the existence of this independent, well-organised institution comes as a surprise. Sadly, it is difficult to identify what the Pinzochere did as the surviving documents offer few details, and very little on the group's self-organisation. We do know that the commercial activity of these women consisted in the manufacture and sale of scapulars, also known as *abitini* or *pazienze*, dedicated to the Virgin. The origin of the scapular lies in the vision of the Virgin that Saint Simon Stock, Prior General of the Carmelites, experienced in England in 1251. The Virgin and Child appeared to him and gave him the scapular of Carmel that from then on became the order's emblem.

The term scapular derives from the mediaeval Latin *scapulare*, itself related to *scapula*, or shoulderblade. Initially, the scapular was part of the dress worn by religious groups such as the Oblates, the Third Orders and others. A sort of sleeveless bodice that slipped over the head, it gradually shrank in size until it was merely two small panels of cloth worn on chest and back. Supported by strips of cloth over the shoulders, these two medallions were worn under the habit in contact with the skin as devotional objects of protection, embroidered with the images of saints.

The scapular was at first considered appropriate only for the poorer, minor religious orders. It was also distributed to members of the Confraternities, and later to all believers, among whom it became increasingly popular. It was seen as a way to obtain spiritual benefits and shelter from the adversities of life through the assistance of the Virgin or a protecting saint, whose likenesses were embroidered on the object with mottoes, verses from Scripture, symbols and prayers.

Ceiling of the Sala Capitolare with oil on canvas paintings by Giambattista Tiepolo.

14 Giambattista Tiepolo,
Angel Bearing Lilies and Putto
Offering the Scapular,
detail, 1743
oil on canvas, 164 x 280 cm.

Of all the scapulars manufactured in many different places for various cults, the one that was most popular was from Madonna dei Carmini, produced at Venice in huge numbers for very many years. It was sold in the houses along the street that became known as the Calle delle Pazienze, which ran along the left side of the church.

The congregation of women who made scapulars was already in existence in the fourteenth century. Members were regular attenders at the church of the Carmini, where according to tradition there was an altar dedicated to the Visitation of the Virgin. Some of the poorer,

30

older or more infirm members had found shelter and protection at a hospice in Santa Margherita. The modestly proportioned building had been donated by an otherwise unidentified Luigi Velmo, who had wanted to help the women. The donation proves the existence of a devotional and welfare association that over the years had grown, expanding its economic potential with the income from the manufacture and sale of scapulars.

The need to reorganise this ancient women's association became pressing in the late sixteenth century. The group was by then in decline, financially and as an institution, and it was too closely linked to the monastic order. Above all, however, it was desired that the ancient tradition of devotion should continue.

At the initiative of a group of citizens, a new Confraternity was formed, which absorbed the women's group that had formed part of the Carmelite organisation. The new Scuola dei Carmini, in deference to the monastic order on which it was based, took the Virgin as its devotional symbol and the Marian scapular as the distinctive mark of the institution, indicating that the wearer was a Carmelite.

In late 1593, the promoters of the new Confraternity prompted the prior of the monastery to ask Stefano Chizzola, General of the Carmelite order, for permission to install at the church their recently constituted lay Scuola di Devozione dedicated to the Madonna del Carmelo (or Madonna dei Carmini). Approval of the proposal was quick to arrive from the Order's ecclesiastical authorities. At the beginning of the following year, the Scuola had already been formed, and its Mariegola was in operation.

The Scuola was thus from 1594 officially able to use part of the church, in the righthand nave, and an altar for its own services and for the assemblies of its elected representatives. Three years before its formal recognition by the Council of Ten, the Scuola was already active as an institution, performing devotional and welfare activities in public and in private.

Inside the church, the second altar on the right was set aside for the Scuola, which for the occasion, and at its own expense, rebuilt it "richer and more modern", albeit in wood to keep the costs down. The friars also rented to the Scuola the space in the righthand aisle in front of the altar, from the line of the main façade on the *campo* (square) to the entrance to the sacristy.

The agreement was stipulated on 3 March 1595 and the new altar was dedicated to the Virgin of Carmel, replacing the previous dedication to Santa Maria Elisabetta.

The altarpiece portraying the *Virgin in Glory Bestowing the Scapular on Saint Simon Stock* was donated by the artist Pace Pace, a follower of Titian and one of the many members elected to form the first Banca.

In June of the same year, the Carmelite friars also gave the Scuola permission to use a modest area that had previously housed an administrative office in the monastery itself. The position of the room posed serious practical problems, almost certainly because there was a right of way through it.

The situation led to a further move, again to a room rented from the friars, this time in the monastery itself.

Despite the difficulties encountered at the time, and subsequently, in the search for premises, the Brothers of the Carmini showed no intention of moving away from the monastery or the Santa Margherita area, where they continued to look for suitable headquarters. Over the years, there had evidently grown up a close relationship between the members of the Scuola and the friars, as well as the residents of the area, many of whom were enrolled in the Confraternity.

The executives of the Scuola dei Carmini, like those of the more ancient Scuole before them, were committed

to finding and purchasing a suitable site where they could build a permanent, independent headquarters. The problem became increasingly urgent because the Scuola's numbers and activities were growing. The precarious situation the Confraternity had been in for too long after its foundation could no longer be tolerated and an emblematic, physical mark of the Scuola's presence, and of its activities in the life of the city, had to be made. The historian Comoli confirms that the new premises made available by the Carmelites in June 1599 were so ill-suited for the Scuola's needs that the Council of Ten itself intervened to convince the Prior to grant the

13 Giambattista Tiepolo, *Angel with Scrolls and Putti Holding the Mariegola of the Scuola,* detail, 1743 oil on canvas, 164 x 280 cm.

13 Giambattista Tiepolo,
*Angel with Scrolls and
Putti Holding the Mariegola
of the Scuola,*
detail, 1743
oil on canvas, 164 x 280 cm.

Confraternity a site that was more appropriate. Such a location appears to have been identified soon afterwards and the two parties agreed terms for a lease. The contract concerned the "negotiating and composing and equipping of the buying and selling site near the Scuola on the campo" dei Carmini, on the western side, adjacent to the monastery. The "buying and selling" refers to the presence of a small shopkeepers' trade association which had moved into new premises shortly before. Although negotiations had not yet been completed, the Scuola had already put forward its plans for the conversion of the site. These included opening a door onto the campo, and two windows to illuminate the interior, on the part of the wall that was to become the façade of a small Sala Capitolare facing the square.

The friars, however, had doubts about ceding the premises and above all about the proposal to restructure the façade. The Carmelites may have viewed the changes as prejudicial to the future use of the site, whereas some of the Scuola's members thought the friars' financial demands excessive. In the end, nothing came of the project. Nevertheless, relationships between Scuola and church continued to be good, especially on religious matters, although the question of a room at the monastery was more controversial. In early 1604, a new agreement was drawn up for the concession of a different space, which had previously been used by the friars as a chancellery. An annual rent of two scudos was laid down, in addition to an initial, non-returnable payment of twenty scudos to the monastery. Later, the Brothers of the Scuola abandoned the idea of housing their activities in the monastery buildings alone, and began to look seriously at the possibility of finding other premises. They widened their search to include privately owned sites and houses, provided that these were in the Santa Margherita dei Carmini area.

On 10 April 1624, two Brothers from the Scuola, Franco Fondi and Alessandro Perca, were appointed to look into the question.

The two new delegates had a free hand to initiate purchase negotiations and, if necessary, appoint technical consultants and commission plans. These would then be presented to the chancellery, which would take steps to have them approved by the Chapter. The nomination of Fondi and Perca shows that the move was being taken seriously. A few weeks later, the pair were able to report that an area very close to the church, on the opposite side of the *calle*, or street, was available for purchase. They had started negotiations with the Civran and Bolani families, heirs of the Guoros, who lived in a house looking onto the Campo dei Carmini and who owned a number of adjacent lots stretching as far as the canal. On 24 July 1625, almost thirty years after its official recognition by the Council of Ten, the Scuola dei Carmini at last look possession of an area on which to build its own premises. The new erection would be independent of the monastery and enjoy great social prestige. The area was occupied by several elderly, unassuming edifices adjudged to be of little value. These were swiftly demolished to make way for a project that appeared to be definitive. Nevertheless, subsequent developments saw the Confraternity forced to manage its affairs in the new premises in the midst of lengthy litigation with the family from which the site had been acquired.

Two other Brothers, Cristoforo Martelli and Guidotto Guidotti, were nominated to assist Fondi and Perca in the purchase, which was completed a year later, on 14 September 1626.

The same members were assigned the task of completing the necessary formalities and commissioning the plans for the new building from reputable technicians and architects. The proposal adjudged most appropriate for the needs of the Scuola was to be selected, approved and built as quickly as possible. It was decided that the time limit for presentation of the project would be one month. However, it was nearly a year before the chancellery held an extraordinary meeting to approve the building of the new premises. The date was 2 July 1627. In fact, the area that had been purchased was not entirely unencumbered. At the corner of the public highway, there stood a pharmacy called Alle Tre Frecce (The Three Arrows), over which the owner lived. According to one of the many conjectures about the Scuola's design, it is likely that the architect envisaged being able to make use of the entire perimeter, and elaborated his project for the whole building,

including the sector that was not yet accessible. A document from the time, referring to a scale drawing or model, shows the corner rooms, including the upper-floor Albergo hall, in all the detail of a proposal for construction. The dimensions specified largely concur with those of the building we see today.

The surface area for the projected construction was slightly rectangular and stood in the corner formed by the junction of the *rio terrà* (infilled canal) "della Scoazzera" and the calle that came to be known as "della Scuola", on the main route between Campo Santa Margherita and Campo dei Carmini. The new Scuola's marble façades were erected on these two public thoroughfares, the south-facing front being considered the main entrance.

14 Giambattista Tiepolo, *Angel Bearing Lilies and Putto Offering the Scapular,* detail, 1743 oil on canvas, 164 x 280 cm.

Giambattista Tiepolo (detail, **14**).

Thereafter, however, it was difficult to maintain the planned unity of architecture, and equally arduous to complete the design and construction of the new structure. Work only came to an end many years later, when disputes over the building's alleged irregularities were settled and the corner occupied by the pharmacy finally became accessible. These vicissitudes had a detrimental effect on the building's unity, influencing the manner, schedule and costs of completion. It could reasonably be claimed, however, that the solutions adopted for the exterior and for the interior by the various architects and clerks of works, including modifications made while building was in progress, achieved, if not unity, at least a monumentality worthy of the Scuola's image.

The design of the new building was commissioned from a certain Francesco Caustello, an individual of whom precisely nothing is known today. The first mention of this building "technician", or decorator, emerged from the archive researches published by Comoli in 1904.

Work on the site did not start until 1628, and took advantage of a first allocation of 8,000 ducats approved on 21 September 1627. The builders were instructed to follow the approved plans in every respect. Any variations would have to be discussed and approved by the Scuola before being implemented.

It is certain that work began but building was interrupted almost at once by the terrible outbreak of plague that was sweeping Venice at the time. The population fell by more than one third and the entire city suffered its awful effects. The epidemic spread quickly and intensely, not just in Venetian territory but also across Italy and the rest of Europe. Business came to a standstill in many sectors as workers died, fell ill, or left for safer surroundings.

It took almost two years before business, and life in general, at Venice began to get back to normal.

Building work, too, restarted on the Carmini site and further budget allocations were made. The first of these was released in May 1630 and annual grants continued to be made until 1638. The amounts involved were significant, ranging from 2,000 to 4,000 ducats each year, until finally the considerable sum of 22,000 ducats had been appropriated. This information, confirmed by many documentary records, is also contained in an article in the Mariegola rewritten in 1638 by the Provveditori di Comun magistrates. Work had certainly not been completed by that date for further allocations were necessary, most of which were reserved specifically for the interiors. Records show that by 1644, construction was nearly finished. In the meantime, expenses had risen further to reach a total of 35,000 ducats. The original designer, Caustello, intended to locate the two largest and most prestigious spaces, with walls running along three sides of the perimeter, on the right-hand side of the rectangle. They would thus have occupied the entire length facing onto Campo Santa Margherita, and stretched along almost two thirds of the site's depth. Those spaces were, of course, the Chapel and the Sala Capitolare on the floor above. In the area facing Campo dei Carmini, Caustello put the sacristy and the elaborate staircase on the ground floor. Above, he put the Sala dell'Archivio and the Sala dell'Albergo. The latter, as we have seen, was to be in the corner area still occupied by the pharmacy.

The heavy expense of the construction programme occasioned delays in progress, but did not jeopardise the work's overall composition. The structural parts of the building had been put in place by the end of 1636, when the Scuola could claim that only "finishing" elements remained, although we might regard some of them, such as the floors and window fittings, as important. Furnishings like the wooden panels and benches along

Giambattista Tiepolo (detail, **13**).

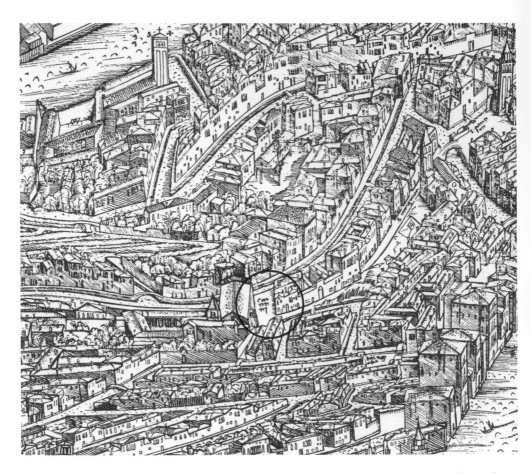

Jacopo de' Barbari,
Prospective plan of Venice,
detail, wood engraving, 1500.
(Museo Correr, Venice).

the walls of the rooms also had to be installed. If the window fittings had still to be put in place, we can assume that the marble façades and their architectural embellishments had already been erected, at least in the sections that face onto the two *calli* (streets).

From the start, construction was at the mercy of factors that had nothing to do with building work itself, but which nevertheless greatly affected progress.

The Guoro family, which lived on the canal side of Campo dei Carmini, and its heirs the Civran and Bolani families, were the former owners of the area purchased by the Scuola, and of other adjacent lots. They took legal action to contest many alleged irregularities in the Scuola building, and to lodge complaints about failure to respect the rights of neighbouring properties, claiming substantial damages as a result. Litigation went before the competent magistrates, the Giudici del-l'Ufficio del Proprio, who carried out an on-site inspection to establish the facts of the case. The complaints regarded the placing of the foundations and the thickness of the walls, which were alleged to encroach illegally upon the shared boundaries.

The height of the new Scuola was another bone of contention.

After their site visit, the Giudici del Proprio ruled in favour of the Scuola. Indeed, they invited the Confraternity to continue construction work, rejecting the plaintiffs' application for the expensive demolition of the disputed sections. The Scuola had pointed out in writing that the building was being erected for devotional and charitable purposes, denying that there were personal interests of any kind involved. The architectural merit of the edifice would beautify the city. Some of the irregularities alleged in relation to the steps at the entrance were admitted, but the discrepancy was minimal and did not exceed fifteen centimetres. It was in any case irrelevant for the purposes of the complaint, particularly as the irregularity impinged upon the public highway and not the area of private property. Another document, dated 25 November 1636, reveals a further detail that may have been crucial to the resolution of the controversy. In that year, the Scuola acquired all the Civran Bolani properties adjoining the inner perimeter, "in order to be able to complete work on the Scuola", thus removing the possibility of legal action to oppose the construction.

Before restarting work on the Scuola building, the Confraternity again applied to the Giudici di Piovego magistracy for permission to modify the previous designs of the south-facing façade by reducing the number of architectural features. The alterations appear to have involved the bases of the paired columns, now only eight in number instead of fourteen, which marked off the spaces of the ground-floor façade, enclosing a series of alternating portals and windows. This second architectural plan, introduced at this juncture by the building's designer, is difficult to describe from the surviving documents. In particular, there is doubt about the number of elements involved, in comparison with the edifice that was actually built and survives to the present day.

The area that the Scuola was able to purchase between 1628 and 1635 was actually greater than that envisaged by the initial project. The new site extended behind, and to the side of, the edifice itself. For reasons of financial policy, because the designs had already been approved, because the land was purchased in several stages, and also because times were changing, the newly acquired site was not exploited to build extensions to the Scuola. Instead, the original compact, restrained volume was preferred. Its architectural presence is almost modest in comparison with the formal grandeur of Venice's other Scuole Grandi, such as San Rocco, San Marco and the Scuola della Carità. The final design, and subsequent building programme, were not modified to take account of the newly acquired spaces, whose commercial use was maintained. The additional space was subject to general town-planning criteria and had to include a number of residential units for the Scuola's employees, as well as shops that appear to have already been there, including a butcher's, a haberdasher's and a delicatessen.

The Scuola building must therefore have already been erected and, in practice, operational. Brothers may have had to walk on wooden boards during meetings in the first-floor Sala Capitolare, or on bare earth when they were celebrating and hearing mass in the ground-floor

Chapel. The altar may not have been finished. But almost all the rest of the building must have been structurally in place, not forgetting the Sala dell'Archivio and perhaps the Sala dell'Albergo over the pharmacy. The staircase, comprising the two flights facing the Carmini, was certainly complete. The arrangement of the interior is confirmed by the information, dating from November 1636, that a significant consignment of church ornaments was purchased for religious services. Chalices, monstrances, chasubles and censers arrived for use in the Scuola's religious celebrations, both at the monastery church and in the Chapel of the new edifice.

Giambattista Tiepolo,
Faith,
(detail. **15**).

The Scuola building was officially inaugurated in October 1638. This public occasion is further evidence that by that date, the new premises were safe and practicable. Nor should we forget that the painting of the *Assumption* by Padovanino for the ceiling of the Sala Capitolare was already in place that year, some time before the inauguration. The stucco on the ceiling around the painting had also been completed. This means that work on not only the structure but also several sectors of the decoration had progressed, and in some cases been completed, along with the floors, windows and window fittings that we have seen were previously in the early stages of installation. A declaration from after 1644 states that the building was "in an excellent state of perfection as can be seen, for it lacks only some decorations, which will be made up in daily work patches", providing telling evidence that work was by then nearly complete. Further interventions in the following years would concern only interior fittings and embellishments, as emerges from the subsequent invoices paid by the Scuola for decoration.

Finally, in 1667, the Scuola had the long-awaited opportunity to add the final touches to its new premises.

On 24 July, in very hot, humid weather, the Scuola's General Chapter met in the hall on the first floor after hearing mass in the chapel below. The meeting was called to deliberate the purchase of the house on the corner where, as we have noted, the Alle Tre Frecce pharmacy operated. For many years, it had been run by a now-elderly pharmacist who lived over the shop and the edifice reached roughly the level of the Scuola's first floor. The ancient, dilapidated building, owned by a Venetian noble, Candiano Bolani, is mentioned in the Confraternity's archives as "adjacent to our Scuola and in danger of collapse".

Wedged into the corner section of the Scuola, the pharmacy had for almost forty years prevented the premises of the Confraternita dei Carmini from taking on its definitive configuration, blocking any other construction work and also causing serious damage to the fabric of the Scuola itself.

The Chapter's decision was unanimous. The Scuola would purchase the part of the site it still required, and would pay Bolani the agreed price. Three building professionals and lawyers, Contin, Protti and Torelli, were also nominated to negotiate the purchase, which we know had still not been completed in July 1668. On 19 August, however, the administrative act affirming the legitimate transfer of ownership to the Scuola must have been in force. The Scuola instructed the same commission to begin the procedures that would complete the remaining building operations, and in particular the two façades that were unfinished.

One of the main contributors to the substantial expense involved was the noble Barbaro Badoer, who had passed away in July of the same year. His generous bequest helped greatly to offset the cost of the work.

Towards the end of 1668, a few days before Christmas, the Scuola's legal representatives were given authority to "build in compliance with the drawings and accompany the whole front façade". In other words, the

Lodovico Ughi,
Plan of Venice,
detail, engraving, 1729.
(Museo Correr, Venice).

commission could complete the main façade, echoing and "accompanying" the compositional rhythms of the existing section in the new part, to maintain the overall architectural unity of the frontage.

The side facing the Carmini was the one concerned, although this was not specified. In all likelihood, it was regarded as the secondary façade, and therefore not important enough to be named explicitly.

After nearly half a century, it was at last possible to consider how the Scuola dei Carmini was going to appear in its final form.

The architect Tommaso Contin came from a family of builders who had moved to Venice in the latter half of the sixteenth century. Contin was commissioned to draft a detailed report before work started on the final stage of the building. Later, supervision of the work, and the design of some of the interiors, was assigned to the most celebrated Venetian architect active in the city at the time, Baldassare Longhena. Born in Venice in

1598, Longhena was a leading exponent of the Baroque artistic ideal and the creator of many of Venice's major buildings, the most significant of which was the votive basilica of the Salute, built after the terrible plague of 1630. In the same year when he was working at the Carmini, and held the public post of Proto della Repubblica, Longhena also began work on the nearby Palazzo Bon-Rezzonico at San Barnaba on the Grand Canal.

The Longhena scholar Camillo Semenzato dates the architect's work on the Scuola to between 1668 and 1670, which was a particularly busy period for the great man. Nevertheless, Longhena accepted the commission,

Plan of the ground floor
of the Scuola Grande dei Carmini.

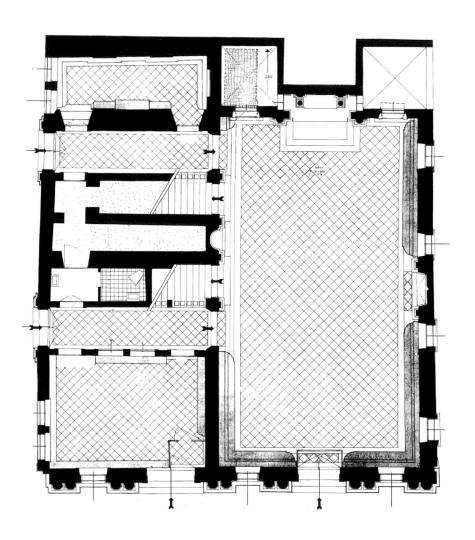

which must have seemed to him a very modest intellectual challenge. It was restricted to the completion of
the façades in the corner area, where he was obliged to
continue the same architectural design that had been
commenced, and left incomplete, forty years previously.
Several documents appear to support those who claim
that Longhena's intervention on the exterior of the
Scuola was very limited indeed, and in no way decisive
for the building as a whole. Some commentators also
point out that Longhena was only appointed to supervise construction. This view is in disagreement with
those who assert that Longhena actually designed at
least the main façade, basing the claim on an evalua-
tion of its composition and style. Unfortunately, there
are no records to back up the thesis.

In late 1668, a commission comprising Mattio Tumitan,
Simone Nardi and Iseppo Caliari, probably members of

*Transverse section
of the Scuola Grande dei Carmini.*

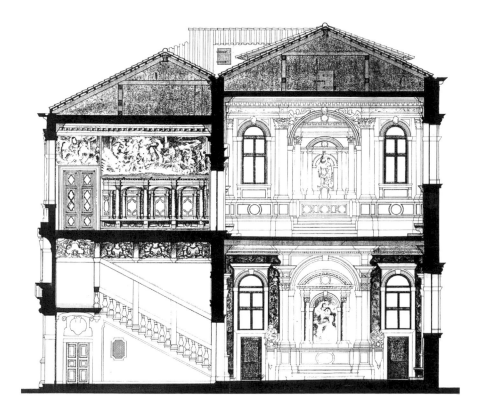

the Scuola, signed a contract on the association's behalf with Gerolamo Liviani and Santo di Barbieri, stonemasons and suppliers of stone materials. The contractors undertook to complete the two façades in conformity with the existing sections. The document stipulates that "... the same order must be continued on the front (facing Campo Santa Margherita), and on the side facing the church (Campo dei Carmini), and the one should be joined to the other up to the corner of the pharmacy. The two façades should meet those already in place at that point from top to bottom, up to the right of the moulding of the upper order". The text continues, ordering that "all work should be carried out in conformity with the model made by S. Baldisera Longhena, Protto of this City". It is from this last phrase, quite apart from any other conjectures, that the attribution to Longhena of the Scuola's south façade derives.

Relief drawing of the western façade of the Scuola Grande dei Carmini.

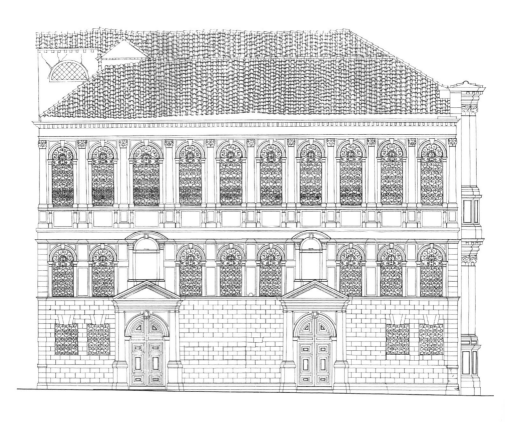

The document we have quoted, however, makes very clear the situation at the time. Above all, it stipulates the way in which work was to be carried out. We see that the righthand part of the main façade, corresponding to the Sala Capitolare and the Chapel underneath, was already complete. The lefthand sector had to be completed as far as the corner, to meet the other façade. This was considered secondary or lateral, and had to be finished on the right, up to the moulding. The note does not appear to admit other interpretations. In any case, we have to suppose that there was a single architectural design for the entire width of the building, from corner to corner.

Interpretation of the existing work's stylistic language does not exclude the presence of elements typical of Longhena's taste, which by the seventh decade of the seventeenth century had become part of

Relief drawing of the southern façade of the Scuola Grande dei Carmini.

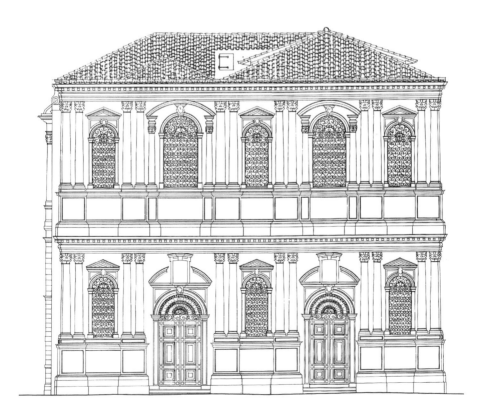

contemporary Venetian Baroque. Nevertheless, we should remember that the design of the obscure architect Caustello dated from as early as 1627-28, whereas Longhena was now consolidating his reputation with the stupendous church of the Salute. Yet comparisons with other works by Longhena from the years around 1670 are unconvincing. We need only mention the façade of the Ospedaletto at Santi Giovanni e Paolo. It is as contradictory, contrived, sculpturesque, fantastical and plastic as the Carmini building is plain, monumentally static and classicising. The only exceptions at the Carmini are one or two widely used Baroque elements such as the marble heads on the keystone of the arches, the open-topped and segmental arches, the height of the base plinths and an insistent striving for effects of light and shade by varying the depth of the various planes. It could be said that the Carmini presents a classical composition enlarged from within, although the interior does nothing more than highlight and emphasise. On the one hand, Caustello seems ahead of his time, and too expertly up to date, whereas Longhena's work looks almost impoverished and simplified. Yet all these often contradictory observations cannot disguise the singular fact that Longhena, who was a celebrated architect and involved at the same time in other, much more ambitious, projects should accept the lowly professional role the Scuola assigned to him, even though it was probably very well paid. The treatment of the two façades presents an obvious, and very substantial, difference of interpretation, both architecturally and stylistically. The two sides are configured in to comply with different urbanistic requirements and internal distributions. The first, facing onto the more open space of Campo Santa Margherita, is compact in volume and acquires a clear feeling of monumentality. In contrast, the side flanking the church is broken up in correspondence to secondary interior spaces, thus attenuating its impact on the local environment. Two distinct interpretations have been implemented to resolve a series of practical problems, and to engage in a new form of "corporate communication". Nevertheless, they remained distinct, kept separate by a compositional language applied to different exterior and interior relationships. After completion, the two façades actually met so that the adoption of two distinct forms of architectural expression made even more apparent their different ideal and practical significance. On one side was a upwards-thrusting monumentality while on the other, we find horizontal fragmentation.

Longhena brought with him a global revision of the Scuola as a building, and completed its construction in compliance with the new concept. Yet it is undeniable that the work reveals an effort of mediation between past and present, however superficially one glances at the differences.

Work on the façades proceeded without any great hurry, for in early 1699, an enclosed shelter was still being erected at the Scuola in Campo dei Carmini. It was to serve as a workshop for the stonemasons who were cutting the pieces for the part of the façade that had still to be finished. The contract laid down that the stonemasons had to comply precisely with the model indicated and provide the stones "... insofar as the competence of the stonemason's profession extends ..." and also supply "... the fine, good Rovigno stones dressed by good and sufficient craftsmen ...".

The total expense was specified and agreed by both parties to be 2,500 ducats, which included the supply, dressing and laying of the stone. Payment was to be made in several instalments at various stages of construction. The builders were also to be given the stones recovered after the demolition of a number of houses

belonging to the Scuola and stored in a small courtyard behind the main Scuola building.

On 10 May 1669, the Chapter met again to approve the entire operation by thirty three votes out of thirty seven. The order was given to demolish the pharmacist's house and shop "... to build and perfect ..." both façades.

At the end of that year, a few days before Christmas, the Scuola's legal representatives were authorised to build to plan the "front" façade in its entirety, that is to complete it, repeating the architectural features already present in the part that had been erected previously. The plans to which reference was made could have been those of the original design, by Caustello, or those drawn up by Baldassare Longhena, who is documented at the Scuola site only in the three-year period from 1668 to 1670, or thereabouts.

Longhena may not even have had any latitude at all with regard to the design. It is thus at best curious that an architect of his fame and skill should have agreed to play the lowly professional role that the Scuola had assigned him, for he was involved at the time in much more ambitious design and building projects. However, we should remember that he was also commissioned for various features in the interior, such as the great staircase, the altars and the entrance portals of the halls.

These reflections have led some scholars to speculate that Longhena may have accepted a commission to design the entire façade complex, demolishing the existing marble structure to erect a different, and more modern, solution. Yet the many surviving records from the period appear to confirm the thesis that Longhena's intervention on the exterior of the Scuola was limited to merely completing the façade, following the lines and themes it had had since the beginning.

Façade of the Scuola Grande dei Carmini facing Campo dei Carmini.

Boy's head on entrance to the Chapel.

In effect, the great man contented himself with acting as a clerk of works.

There may, however, be a third possibility. Longhena may have been commissioned to design the façades – a commission that is unattested in the records – but not in the three-year period we are considering. Longhena may have been active during the early stages of construction at some time prior to 1630, the year of the plague and the suspension of work. What is certain is that the following year, Longhena would be invited, as the winner of the Republic's competition, to design and build the church of Santa Maria della Salute, his most emblematic and important masterpiece.

According to this recently advanced hypothesis, both façades of the Scuola, which were partially built when work was interrupted because of the pharmacy, could have been designed by Longhena right from the start. Many years later, it would have been perfectly reasonable for the Brothers of the Confraternity to summon him to finish the job he had started so many years earlier, when at last the Scuola was able to purchase the corner property and had free access to the remainder of the site. Although none of the sources make any mention of this earlier presence of Longhena at the Carmini, the hypothesis does offer a convincing reply to some of the questions of a stylistic and professional nature that would arise if the great architect's contribution had been restricted to the later three-year period.

It is also very unlikely that Longhena would have been commissioned to make a model for the completion of two façades that were already partially erected. By "model", the committee nominated by the Confraternity appears to have been referring to an existing drawing which had been in the Scuola's possession for some time, and which was to be followed scrupulously in continuation of the part of the structure already in place.

The architectural lines previously laid down were to be reflected in the new construction. In this case, Caustello, previously indicated as the designer, would actually have been merely the builder or contractor for the work, as we have no other indications except for the document.

The Scuola dei Carmini is in that case one of Baldassare Longhena's earliest works in the "modern", or Baroque, style, contemporary with the façades of the Widmann-Foscari, Giustinian-Lolin and Papadopoli-Marcello palazzos, and prior to the reconstruction of the Duomo at Chioggia, which had been destroyed by fire. Confirmation for the thesis comes from a comparison of shared stylistic elements. Some architectural components are common, such as the segmental arches, large bases and boy's heads at the Salute, with their smiling expressions and distinctive hair.

The Scuola must have had some difficulty in its dealings with the pharmacist, who was called Claudio Faresini. As late as March 1671, it was decided "... for the interests of the shop ..." to pay to him a negotiable sum of between one hundred and two hundred ducats, in all likelihood to meet Faresini's demands for compensation for leaving the property. In the meantime, the surfaces of the streets around the Scuola and church were laid, initially with bricks arranged in a herringbone pattern and later with blocks of trachyte similar to those that may be seen today.

When work started under Longhena on the front and side façades, a special committee of three Confraternity members was elected to supervise operations, laying down schedules and procedures with full authority, including over technical and architecture-related decisions. This is the situation described by surviving records, including a very interesting document from 1669. In this context, the Guardian Grande, the Sindaci

Boy's head on side entrance facing church.

(internal auditors) and the officials elected "over the building" laid down that the lefthand section of the façade should include a "... main door conforming to the other (main door) constructed ..." and for the rest "... to adapt ..." to the order that the façade already built presented.

The main façade has two identical, equidistant main doors alternating with three windows. These are imposing features in relation to the extent of the frontage, whose rhythm derives from paired Corinthian half-columns resting on very high, sturdy plinths of super-imposed marble blocks, the top block being highlighted by squaring cornices. An emphatically highlighted string course divides the frontage at mid height and the upper floor repeats the same architectural features alternating with the paired columns. Round arches with male or female heads decorating their keystones are surmounted by triangular pediments in the outer and middle windows, and by segmental arch pediments in the main doors and corresponding upper-storey windows. The open-topped arch of the two main doors leaves enough space for a square niche. In the two upper-storey windows, the arch is unbroken but the moulding at the base, which receives the keystone of the arch underneath, is interrupted. The upper floor picks up the motif of the plinth at the base of the paired columns, their front planes advanced with respect to the windowsills. Their varying depth creates significant areas of light and shade, depending on the position of the sun.

The building is crowned by a double cornice coping and corbel table below the eaves.

The two upper windows over the main doors are wider than the others. Their dual architecture is more complicated, for the pediment is aligned with the side pilasters supporting the window's central arch, which lends a slight sense of perspective. The second façade,

Corner of the two façades
of the Scuola Grande dei Carmini.

facing the calle where the church stands, has a very different architectural rhythm. The organisation in three orders means the elements are smaller in size, and also tends to emphasise the general fragmentation of the surface. Its interpretation is thus less confrontational and impelling.

Summing up, we might say that the Santa Margherita façade "rises up" whereas the Carmini one "distributes" or "articulates" itself in a sequence. Nonetheless, the second façade also presents peaks in the two main doors, whose strongly resurgent pediments are surmounted by niches that stand bereft of statues, today as in the past.

Levelled marble rustication, in proportion to the whole, is the main feature of the ground-floor cladding, forming the base into which the windows are cleanly cut. On the two upper floors, marked off by a light double string course, the succession of circular-arch windows on Corinthian pilaster strips extends without interruption or spatial variation, lending rhythm and continuity.

The first-floor windows are interrupted only by the two niches. They have the sill of the middle landing of the main staircase, marked off at the top by the string course. The atmosphere of the interior is rendered more solemn by the second-floor windows that rise over projecting plinths with elegant Corinthian pilaster strips. They are arranged in a line and separated by the smooth marble of the sills based on the inner line of the wall. Inside, they appear in relation to the floor above the line of the wooden bench seats that grace the side walls.

The corner where the two façades adjoin was tackled in a simplistic, or at least simple, way. The structures, and their respective mouldings, meet edge on and the architect has separated them with a smooth, continuous strip of Istria stone that runs the entire height of the corner. This makes a simulated formal, anonymously expressed, division of the different volumes in the interior. The vertical subdivisions of this part of the building emerge in the different heights of the internal floors, which correspond to the rooms that open onto both the main Santa Margherita façade and the secondary façade opposite the church. At the top is the Sala dell'Albergo, occupying the full height of the floor. The spaces beneath, the long middle landing of the staircase and the superimposed secretary's room and ground-floor reception room, extend to half height. These rooms fully comply with the architectural design on one side while on the other, the compromise to fit them in is apparent in the presence of elements in spaces where they do not belong. The intermediate floor is disguised by the frame that runs through the main door and the last window on the left, and the height of the horizontal structures is extended with respect to their breadth. These and other elements show that the structural aesthetic was not integrated with the original design. The external architectural solutions had to be adapted to the functional layout of the interior plan. In short, the building's location, and the planimetric distribution of the interior, have imposed major variations. The interpretation of the two façades is kept separate visually by the anonymous vertical marble strip. Its presence, although understated, is significant and invites a dual reading.

The seventeenth century was drawing to a close. Events of recent years had been decisive for the architectural definition of the Confraternity's new home. Longhena's contribution was complete, both in the building and outside. The Brothers could now devote their attention with greater concentration to the embellishment of the rooms with valuable paintings, stucco decorations, furniture and fittings.

The Chapel

Preceding pages:
Chapel with altar dedicated to the Virgin of Carmel.

Access to the Chapel from the street is directly through the broad main door on the right, which stands at the top of a short flight of three steps. There is a second entrance through a door on the righthand side of the building in the narrow Calletta del Nonzolo. In the general plan of the Scuola, access to the public highway from the Chapel is also possible through two doors on the opposite side, across two passages that belong to the staircase complex.

The ceremonial plane of the altar, which is built in a shallow niche, is also raised above floor level by three steps.

The Chapel's generally plain, restrained architecture is in the seventeenth-century idiom. The altarpiece (**5** *Virgin of Carmel*, Sante Piatti) occupies the space created by the applied columns in pink Verona stone, surmounted by a segmental-arch tympanum. The whole rests on the wall behind, framed by a more imposing structure. This comprises a broad round arch flanked by fluted half-columns mounted on a pedestal and terminating in an elongated capital. Just under the roof beams, the capital meets the frieze and rectilinear upper moulding.

The arched main door is framed by fluted Corinthian pilaster strips bearing a rectilinear moulding embellished with a strip of grey marble. The same scheme, in a monumental version, was used by the architect – who may have been Longhena – at every structural opportunity on the left side of the hall where the two rising flights of stairs abut. The second upper flight leading from the middle landing to the Sala Capitolare corresponds in width to the central space of the niche, continued architecturally in the lateral doors.

Two lower, architraved lateral doors with the same moulding open onto the two parallel and opposing passages that lead into the Calle della Chiesa and to Campo

6 Nicolò and Giovanni Bambini, *Rest on the Flight into Egypt*, 1733-1739, oil on canvas, 360 x 270 cm.

1 Nicolò and Giovanni Bambini,
The Circumcision of Christ,
1733-1739,
oil on canvas, 360 x 550 cm.

dei Carmini. These portals are arranged as a monumental series but have varying forms and functions. Together, they comprise a significant architectural feature that lends the left wall of the Chapel great structural and decorative prominence, which is further enhanced by its numerous paintings.

The wooden bench seats set in panels along the walls were renovated in the eighteenth century. The marble floor is made up of white and red squares of Istria stone and Verona marble, laid out on the diagonal in the traditional Venetian manner. The two *trionfi* (candleholders) date from the mid eighteenth century. Their bases are in painted and lacquered wood whereas the arms, in gilded wrought iron, flaunt leaf and flower motifs.

Since most of the windows open onto narrow external spaces, a still, muted light filters into the Chapel, lending it an atmosphere conducive to meditation. Painting of the Chapel began in 1728 with Nicolò Bambini (1651-1739), the artist who created the three canvases depicting the theological Virtues, **2** *Faith,* **3** *Hope* and **4** *Charity* (1729), which frame the door leading to the staircase. Work proceeded slowly, and indeed came to a halt for some time, so towards the end of the decade, Nicolò was joined by his son, Giovanni. This quickened the pace of painting, which was completed in 1739. The Bambinis painted some of the works in tandem, including the **1** *Circumcision of Christ* and the **6** *Rest on the Flight into Egypt.* The other paintings – the **9** *Annunciation,* the **7** *Assumption* and the **8** *Angel Bestowing the Scapular* – are by Giovanni Bambini.

The originality of the cycle, which adorns every space on the walls, lies especially in its use of monochrome shades of grey, a highly effective decorative technique. The themes are related to the life of the Virgin, the exaltation of her virtues and praise of the scapular. The *Circumcision,* the largest of the paintings, covers almost twenty square metres.

The staircase and middle landing

The staircase lends structural and, above all, decorative richness in relation to the dimensions of the Scuola as a whole. Originally, it may have comprised just one flight rising from the Chapel to the middle landing. A second flight, arranged parallel to it and running in the opposite direction, reached the Sala Capitolare on the first floor.

The side passage flanking the first flight, which led out onto Campo dei Carmini through the only door that existed before the pharmacy was purchased, took visitors from the entrance into the Sacristy, which abutted onto the same façade at back of the site. The Sacristy has conserved its original seventeenth-century decoration, including the squared stuccoes in the tunnel vaulting and relief mouldings by Abbondio Stazio.

Completion of the staircase is believed to date from the period of Longhena's intervention. A second flight rising from the ground floor was added, flanked by a passage that ran symmetrical to the existing passage on the other side. The new exit was through the second door on the right of the Calle della Scuola façade.

Planimetrically, the whole comprises five parallel, elongated rectangular spaces. The three central ones contain the stairs, leading to the middle landing, which rests on the external wall and extends beyond the two passages flanking the flights. The landing opens into a balustrade that serves the entrances to two facing rooms. One, known as the Treasure Room, is situated over the Sacristy and the other is called the Room of Holy Vestments. Both lie in the corners of the two façades in the upper half of the ground-floor space.

Longhena's inspiration added monumentality and greater functionality to the whole, opening up a succession of perspective and passing spatial visualisations that had not existed previously. These are clearly legible from innumerable points of view, creating a multiple structural effect that offsets the reduced dimensions of the space.

The material used was Istria stone, simply and elegantly dressed, and highlighted by contours cut into the depth.

The pillars on the free side of the lower ascending flights are very robust and the intrados of the arches features a series of sunken square panels. Columned balustrades accompany the stairs, continuing on the landing to provide protection from the well over the passage, which extends up the full height of the staircase.

The tunnel-vault soffit over the stairs, and the square wall spaces, with their slightly segmental arch, of the landing and side passages, were decorated throughout with white and gold stucco. The author of this tasteful, skilfully executed work, completed in 1728 and 1729, was Alvise Bossi and his scheme is generally precise and repetitive.

Alvise Bossi, *detail of the stuccoes in the vaulting of the staircase.*

The first ascending flight of Longhena's monumental staircase.

View of the middle landing of the staircase showing the three flights.

The material has a solid, chunky feel and the movement of the white relief cornices is enhanced by full-figure *putti* (chubby naked boys), angels, mermaids and plumed eagles. The cornices enclose smooth, curved-edged spaces of golden depth and ovals flaunting frescoes, most of which have unfortunately been lost. Sante Piatti's portraits of the theological Virtues on the first flight have, however, survived.

All the geometrical figures are surrounded by floral corollas. The floor of the landing is an inlay of white, red and black marble diamonds, aligned along the shorter diagonal. Abundant, clear light floods in through the windows running along the length of the landing, forcefully bringing out the cornices and figures and burnishing the golden backdrop, which emerges to add a dynamic note of shadow.

The Sacristy and eighteenth-century
walnut bench panels.

The door of the Sala Capitolare
leading to the upper flight
of the staircase.

The doors of the Sala Capitolare.

Sala Capitolare

The most important room in the Scuola dei Carmini, the Sala Capitolare is situated over, and is co-extensive with, the Chapel. Its historic significance derives from the fact that the Capitolo, or Chapter, met here and its artistic merits come from its decorative scheme and the paintings it houses, particularly the splendid contribution of Giambattista Tiepolo in the fifth decade of the eighteenth century.

This is where the Scuola's most important formal ceremonies were held. It is also the room where "original citizens" elected to office in the Confraternity received the honours and distinctions of their exalted social status.

The Sala Capitolare is very well-lit and acquires an almost festive air from light pouring in through windows on three sides.

Preceding pages:
The Sala Capitolare and ceiling decorated by Giambattista Tiepolo.

There are three doors in the lefthand wall, the central one, its triangular tympanum resting on Corinthian half-columns, corresponding to the upper flight of stairs. On this floor, the staircase is central and single, not double as on the lower level. The architecture largely reflects that of the Chapel. An internal arch marks off the tunnel vault of the flight, which offers itself whole to observers in the Sala Capitolare and dominates its space from the closed, parallel boundaries of the side walls. The upwards thrust of the door, which reaches the ceiling cornice, is offset by the less agile lines of the lower side doors. The inner element of their three-part piers forms the architraved surrounding of the door space while the other two rise beyond to meet the segmental-arch, broken-apex pediment. The side doors lead to the Sala dell'Archivio and the Sala dell'Albergo.

The arrangement of the staircase door, and the structure of the altar at the back of the room, present a clear unity of style and a distinctly classical approach, onto which Baroque architectural features have been grafted. Here, too, Longhena's hand can be glimpsed, although there is no documentary evidence to support the hypothesis. He may have collaborated with Antonio Gaspari on the room's design and construction, for we know Gaspari had been one of Longhena's busiest assistants since the building of the church of the Salute.

With Tremignon, Cominelli and Margutti, Gaspari was the artist who proved most adept at absorbing and keeping alive Longhena's artistic legacy in Venice when working on major construction or restructuring projects after the master's death. Nor need we point out that in the dying years of the seventeenth century, Gaspari was rebuilding the nearby Palazzo Zenobio in Fondamenta del Soccorso.

Work had certainly been completed by the end of the century, but too many years separate the Scuola project from the rebuilding of the palazzo for us to be able to link them both to Longhena's pupil. The hypothesis has

The altar in the Sala Capitolare, with its white and gold stucco cupola by Abbondio Stazio.

to be discarded, not least because it is unsupported by documentary evidence. The stylistic flavour of some elements was part and parcel of the taste of the time. The literary interpretation of Baroque's evolution tended in Venice to refashion Palladio-inspired themes from the sixteenth-century instead of developing into an international Rococo.

A great central arch flanked by two windows opens the far wall, creating a niche that comfortably holds the altar complex, including two planes for the officiants, raised respectively by two and three steps.

The arch rests on square-section pillars, flanked by fluted Corinthian half-columns. Bas-relief winged angels adorn the space above the extrados. The altar itself extends over two successive structures that impart a perspective effect, one seeming to be inside the other. The composition is highlighted by the colour contrasts of the white and pink marbles, and by the gilt edging.

The larger triangular tympanum on its high, edged frieze is supported by applied columns and opens onto a second view, with pink Verona marble columns and a segmental-arch tympanum. In the centre is the elegant white marble statue of the ▨ *Virgin and Child Bestowing the Scapular*, completed at the same time by Bernardino da Lugano. The altar is closed along the walls by a marble cornice supporting the vault, which is decorated with exquisite, snow-white stucco putti. These are by Abbondio Stazio, who also worked with Tiepolo on the ceiling of the rest of the Sala Capitolare.

This elegant, generously proportioned stucco complex comprises straight and curved-edged squares of green and pink, with candelabrums and floral festoons in relief, white and gold mouldings, and swarms of winged putti at the corners and in the centre of the squares. The existing decorations were removed to make way for this scheme, which was to provide a context and a background for Tiepolo's stupendous paintings. Abbondio Stazio completed the ceiling and the work in the vault of the altar niche between 1731 and 1733. Ticino-born Stazio was an artist of exceptional imagination and refinement who was active at Venice in the first half of the eighteenth century.

In 1740, the Confraternity stipulated a contract for the gilding of these stuccoes with another decorative artist from Ticino, Carpoforo Mazzetti. He is known to have worked with Stazio on all the latter's surviving Venetian projects, as well as those for which documentary or oral testimony exists. Mazzetti was working at the Scuola in 1742 and in 1743, before the Sala Capitolare was inaugurated and presented to the citizenry that same year. At the inauguration, one corner painting and the largest canvas in the centre had still to be finished.

The previous ceiling was demolished. Completed between 1664 and 1674 by Domenico Bruni, a stuccoer

26 *The altar in the Sala Capitolare and statue of the Virgin and Child.*

26 Bernardino da Lugano,
Virgin and Child Bestowing the Scapular,
marble.

from Brescia, it provided the setting for the painting by Padovanino that hung in the Sala Capitolare until 1740. When Tiepolo's work was installed, the earlier painting was moved to the Albergo room and Bruni's stuccoes were destroyed.

The wooden bench seats along the walls date from the eighteenth century, as do the gold and red wood lamps that were once carried in procession with the Scuola's standard, which was also held here.

Giambattista Tiepolo was invited to complete the painted decoration of the Sala Capitolare ceiling on 21 December 1739. The decision to renovate the room was taken by the Banca while Giambattista Orlandini was Guardian Grande. Tiepolo was to have painted several works to place around Padovanino's vast *Assumption*, executed a few years earlier to adorn the ceiling of the same hall.

Tiepolo accepted, but requested that his decoration should extend into the central area occupied by Padovanino's painting, which he wanted moved and substituted by a work of his own. The themes that were to be treated and the new overall plan for the ceiling were agreed by the artist and the members of the Confraternity, perhaps aided by the Carmelite friars from the neighbouring monastery.

We believe that it was Tiepolo who conceived and first proposed the decorative scheme, and had most

76

Giambattista Tiepolo.
Sincerity,
(detail, **16**).

influence over the final decision. In the centre of the great painting of the Virgin and around it, along the sides, are a further eight works in various formats. The four in the corners portray the cardinal and theological Virtues, related to the Virgin, and four more in the middle feature the symbols of the Scuola, such as the scapular, the Mariegola and the Statutes, borne by angels and putti. The inspiration for the theme, the allegories and the symbols must have come from the *Iconologia* of Cesare Ripa.

It is likely that in 1740, when Tiepolo presented two sketches for the central section, a general drawing or model for the ceiling had already been made and approved. The shapes and sizes of the paintings were defined to enable the insertion of the new works. The second of the two solutions Tiepolo presented was chosen, and would eventually be implemented. This was the delivery schedule that was agreed between artist and patrons: the central painting was to be delivered the same year, if possible before Christmas, and the other eight works were expected in the summer or, at the latest, autumn of the subsequent year. On the basis of the pact, Padovanino's painting was removed to the Sala dell'Albergo almost immediately, where it remained and the ceiling was prepared to receive the Tiepolo cycle that would swiftly be inserted into the appropriate spaces. The Schola, however, had been hopelessly optimistic. In the event, the Confraternity had to wait for nearly ten years before the painting cycle was complete. Despite Tiepolo's promises and goodwill towards the Confraternity, he was working simultaneously on too many projects. The great artist tended to accept commissions, relying on his inventive genius, swift execution and efficient workshop to deliver before the deadlines specified in his contract, but Tiepolo allowed time to slip past while the Scuola attempted to hurry him along by making substantial advance payments. Finally, in 1743, Tiepolo managed to hand over seven of the eight smaller paintings. These were put in place at once on the ceiling, whose stucco decoration had in the meantime been completed. Although the renovated room was incomplete, the Scuola decided to inaugurate it and present the new decoration to the public. Above all, they were keen to show off Tiepolo's masterpiece, which was widely and generously praised. In 1744, the artist finished the last corner painting of the *Virtues*. Another five years were to pass before the Scuola could admire the finished room, when the central painting was inserted in 1749. It was, of course, the most thematically significant of the works, as well as the largest.

10 Giambattista Tiepolo,
The Virgin Bestowing the Scapular on Saint Simon Stock,
detail, 1749
oil on canvas.

13 Giambattista Tiepolo,
Patience, Innocence and Chastity,
detail, 1743
oil on canvas, 235 x 240 cm.

Ceiling

10 Giambattista Tiepolo, *The Virgin and Child Bestowing the Scapular on Saint Simon Stock*, 1749.

The Virgin and Child descend from the clouds amidst angels whose movements and colourful attire express the joyful nature of the composition. The group floats in a deep blue sky tinged pink by the light of the dawning day. The Virgin has the eloquent features of a young woman of the people. Her realistic features are exalted by beauty and she wears a shining white dress under a dark blue cape. Next to the Virgin stands the angel offering the scapular to Saint Simon Stock, who has a white cape over his brown Carmelite habit and is kneeling on the marble step of a temple. Stock, who is portrayed in a classical style, has a long beard and a broad,

10 Giambattista Tiepolo,
*The Virgin Bestowing the Scapular
on Saint Simon Stock,*
oil on canvas, 1749, 533 x 432 cm.

11 Giambattista Tiepolo,
Angel Showing the Scapular to the Souls in Purgatory,
oil on canvas, 1743, 116 x 337 cm.

15 Giambattista Tiepolo,
Faith, Hope and Charity, oil on canvas, 1743, 235 x 240 cm. Faith holds a cross and chalice, Hope an anchor, and Charity is escorted by two putti.

12 Giambattista Tiepolo,
Angel Saving a Devotee of the Virgin Falling from Scaffolding,
oil on canvas, 1743, 116 x 337 cm.

13 Giambattista Tiepolo,
Patience, Innocence and Chastity,
oil on canvas, 1743, 235 x 240 cm. Patience is an old woman with a cross, Innocence is accompanied by a lamb, and Chastity, seen from behind, has a riddle in her hand.

17 Giambattista Tiepolo,
Fortitude and Justice,
oil on canvas, 1743, 235 x 240 cm.
Fortitude, leaning on a column
and accompanied by a lion,
holds a helmet. Justice has a
sword and scales.

bare forehead. His face is that of an elderly man, his expression concentrated and attentive. Behind, a second angel offers succour and invites him to pray.

The lower part of the vision expands to reveal souls suffering in Purgatory among the bones of the dead on the gravestones of uncovered tombs.

The four rectangular paintings to the sides of the central work depict angels and putti.

The putti in the first two paintings hover in the clear, bright air of a blue sky. The reflected sunlight faintly tinges pink the cotton-soft clouds that support the angels. In the other two works, the characters of the narrative fill the space more solidly, yet still convey the idea

of airiness and floating in the void. The four corner paintings depict allegorical female figures of the theological and cardinal Virtues, as well as other spiritual attitudes, all referring to the Virgin. The figures are on high cornices of ancient temples set against deep, open skies that, as in the previous paintings, burst through the physical barrier of the ceiling.

Each of the female figures carries the traditional symbols of her specific virtue.

16 Giambattista Tiepolo, *Prudence, Sincerity, and Temperance*, oil on canvas, 1744, 235 x 240 cm. Prudence has a snake wound round one arm and a mirror, Sincerity holds a dove, and Temperance is pouring water from a jug.

Walls

Over the panelling on the walls is a series of paintings whose dark tonalities are characteristic of Venetian seventeenth-century tenebrism. They complete the Sala Capitolare's decoration, complementing Tiepolo's luminous ceiling cycle.

19 Antonio Zanchi,
The Miracle of the Boy and the Well, c. 1665.

The episode refers to the Virgin's miraculous intervention to save a boy who fell down a well. He was trapped there for eight days because no one was able to pull him out. The group in the foreground is full of movement. Two sturdy men are helping the boy out of the well and handing him over to his mother. She is gazing heavenwards, where an angel accompanies the Virgin and Child. A strong sense of naturalism is combined with the artifice of the light that falls on the figures in the foreground.

20 Antonio Zanchi,
The Virgin Heals the Prince of Sulmona, c. 1665.

The subject is another miracle performed by the Virgin, when she healed a prince who suffered a serious spear wound during a tournament. This canvas is also noteworthy for the violence of the light illuminating the group of figures bearing the injured prince. The tonalities of the landscape are very dark, as is the sky in which the Virgin appears.

21 Anonymous, *A Sick Man is Healed When the Virgin Intercedes*, seventeenth century.

The dark, tragedy-laden atmosphere emphasises the man's suffering before the Virgin intervenes and he makes a miraculous recovery.

22 Amedeo Enz,
Paul V Greeting the Spanish Ambassador.

Paul V (1605-21) was a resolute protector of the Carmelite order, to which he granted numerous indulgences.

19 Antonio Zanchi,
*The Miracle of the Boy
and the Well*, 1665 ca.,
oil on canvas, 325 x 275 cm.

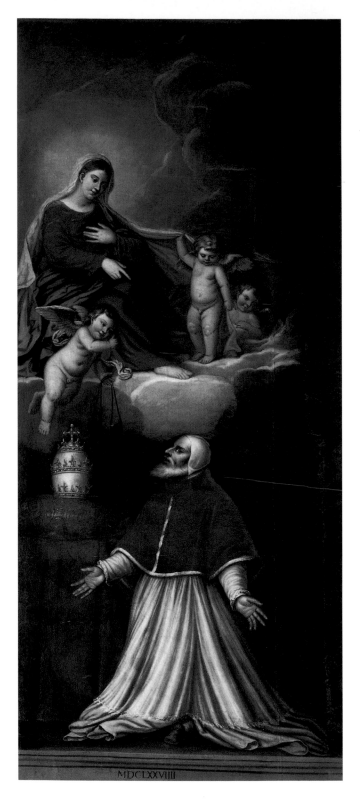

MDCLXXVIIII

23 Anonymous,
Pope John XXII Receiving the Scapular, 1679.
oil on canvas, 330 x 145 cm.

24 Gregorio Lazzarini,
Adoration of the Magi,
detail, 1704
oil on canvas, 330 x 139 cm.

In the painting, a priest next to the pontiff has a scapular. A friar in the Carmelite habit can be seen behind.

23 Anonymous, *Pope John XXII Receiving the Scapular*, 1679. The pope (1316–34) kneels before the Virgin, who appears to him from the clouds accompanied by angels, one of whom is bearing the scapular. The episode illustrated is the vision of the Virgin the pontiff experienced during his struggle in 1322 with the emperor, Ludwig IV, called the Bavarian. The Virgin asked the pope to protect the Carmelites and encourage devotion to the scapular.

24 Gregorio Lazzarini, *The Adoration of the Magi*, 1704. This large-scale composition has a wealth of characters. The Magi, with their pages and servants, are in the centre of the scene, paying homage and offering gifts to the Holy Child, who is held by a kneeling Saint Joseph. The Virgin stands on the extreme right of the picture, observing the scene. There are buildings behind the figures. Through a large archway, we can see a light-filled rural scene, crowded with country folk, animals and vegetation. The general atmosphere is calm and relaxed, but the scene comes to life in the gestures of the figures, especially the Magi themselves, and in the brushwork of their shimmering attire.

25 Gregorio Lazzarini, *The Angels Invite the Shepherds to Adore Jesus*, 1704. The painting is placed at either side of the staircase door and above the entrances to the Sala dell'Archivio and Sala dell'Albergo. The shepherds kneel before Christ as a host of angels appear to urge them to pray from the clouds. The scene is related to the previous painting by a winged angel indicating the Child.

Sala dell'Archivio

The Sala dell'Archivio was set aside as an archive for the Scuola's documents. It was also used as an administration office. Well-integrated and unitary in design, it contains a wide range of important works of art and furnishings.

The monumental Istria stone door corresponds to the marble door in the Sala Capitolare. Classical in concept, it has a rectilinear architrave, frieze and projecting triangular tympanum, whose peak grazes the wooden cornice of the ceiling. On the opposite side, a continuous series of arched windows looks out onto Campo dei Carmini, making the room remarkably well lit.

The walnut panels and benches along the walls are a major decorative feature, their cadence dictated by twelve caryatid-type figures, both male and female, carved with remarkable artistic sensitivity and eloquence of form. Each square is marked off by an elaborate cornice of festoons and volutes that leave the internal space smooth and flat. The back panels are capped by a two-tier carved corbel table. The brackets and sections below the bench are also carved.

The desk is an original piece of working furniture, as is the closet behind. The compartments rest on the back wall and the doors open to reveals the ancient shelving where papers and other documents were stored. On almost the entire length of the far side, the line of benches extends more than a metre beyond the threshold of the door leading to the Sala dell'Albergo to hide the wooden stairs leading to the attic.

It is a difficult task to decide who created this superb piece of wooden sculpture. Superbly expressive and skilfully carved, it is obviously the work of a gifted artist. There is no repetition, even in the detail of the many figures. Comparisons with similar works from the period

insistently suggest the name of Giacomo Piazzetta, a sculptor and wood carver from Pederobba, a village in the province of Treviso. In the latter half of the seventeenth century, Piazzetta was particularly active in Venice, where he had moved and where he died in the late seventeenth or early eighteenth century.

In 1664, restructuring started at the monastery of San Domenico at Santi Giovanni e Paolo, supervised by Baldassare Longhena. The library was totally renovated and in 1670, Longhena called in Piazzetta to carve the sumptuous wooden ceiling, still in place except for the figures of the "heretics", which unfortunately were removed and sold off in the last century. Happily, they were later acquired on the antiquarian market by the Victoria and Albert Museum in London, where they remain to this day. Comparison of the Carmini ceiling with the well-documented Dominican library, where Piazzetta worked until 1674, makes it possible, and credible, that he also carved the figures for the Sala dell'Archivio and the rest of the wooden decoration. It is likely that the male figures represent the prophets Daniel, Jeremiah, Isaiah and Ezekiel. The female carvings are probably women from the Old Testament.

Apart from his carvings, Giacomo Piazzetta is know for being the father of the Giambattista Piazzetta who earned fame as a painter at Venice, where he was born in 1683. Giambattista's works include the canvas of *Judith and Holophernes* **41** next to the door of the Sala dell'Albergo.

The deep carved wood caissons of the lacunar ceiling have high raised edges that frame a series of oval paintings, completed between 1749 and 1753 by Giustino Menescardi, to a scheme by Gaetano Zompini. The ceiling was completed before the paintings were installed and, in compliance with eighteenth-century tastes, the decorative motifs are very elaborate.

Despite this, they still manage to suggest the Mannerism of the late sixteenth century.

Although documentation is lacking, it is reasonable to suppose that the whole of the ceiling was completed in the 1770s, under Longhena's supervision, and this it was this structure into whose predefined compartments Zompini inserted his paintings.

The ceiling was constructed and carved in such a manner as to produce deep caissons and a riot of floral motifs, volutes, festoons, friezes and heads of winged putti. The moulding that runs along all four sides features corbels with rose decorations in the intervening spaces. The overall colouring of the ceiling has taken on a browner hue than it originally had, giving it a very rich wood feel. However, we should not forget that the

structure must originally have been gilded all over, with the usual variations of tone and treatment we find in other works of the same type.

The floor, too, is worthy of mention for its white, pink, grey and black marble inlays. It was installed at about the same time as the ceiling. The pattern is geometrical, two-coloured strips outlining hexagonal, oval or round compartments with simple or multiple star motifs. The alternating colours simulate a relief effect, like light and shade, or rather lend a three-dimensional volume. Here, too, we can note the continuation in new shapes and patterns of a sixteenth-century tradition, recovered and re-interpreted, but very much present.

Giacomo Piazzetta (?),
Wooden bench panels with carved figures in the Sala dell'Archivio.

The wooden ceiling of the Sala dell'Archivio. The iconographic scheme is by Gaetano Zompini.

Ceiling

27 Giustino Menescardi, *The Virgin Appears to the Prophet Elijah on Mount Carmel*, 1749-1753.

The prophet Elijah, the figure who inspires the Carmelite order, venerated the Virgin on Mount Carmel, where towards the end of the twelfth century, the crusading priest Bertoldo of Calabria settled with a group of

followers to dedicate his life to prayer and contemplation in a secluded hermitage. The prophet is portrayed kneeling in prayer for rain after three years of drought. The Virgin appears in a cloud to reassure Elijah that his prayers will soon be answered. The symbolic significance of the episode refers to the Virgin's contribution to the rebirth of hope in a land rendered arid by sin.

The other compartments, beginning with the oval above the cupboard, contain portraits of the Sibyls by Giustino Menescardi. We see the Tiburtine, Delphic, Cumaean, Chaldean, Samian, Libyan, Eritrean, Samian, Phrygian and Hellespontine Sibyls, the last two depicted together on the same canvas. In the Christian tradition, they predict the blows to Christ during the Passion, the Crown of Thorns, the Nativity at Bethlehem, the arrival of the Magi, the Stable, the Advent of the Redeemer, the Annunciation to the Virgin, Mary Suckling Jesus, the Resurrection and so on. The Sibyls of antiquity were prophetesses associated with oracles. All the paintings, like those on the walls and in the next room, were completed between 1749 and about 1753.

29 Giustino Menescardi,
Samian Sibyl,
1749-53
oil on canvas, 65 x 175 crn.

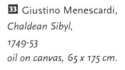

33 Giustino Menescardi,
Chaldean Sibyl,
1749-53
oil on canvas, 65 x 175 cm.

Walls

37 Giustino Menescardi, *Abigail's Offer*, 1749-1753.
The beautiful Abigail is portrayed kneeling before David and offering him food and wine to placate his anger. The king shows his appreciation by putting his sword back in its sheath as a token of peace. King David was very angry and threatening a massacre because shortly before, Abigail's husband Nabal had refused to supply provisions for the royal entourage encamped in the Judaean desert. The two protagonists are surrounded by many other figures. There are soldiers on David's side while handmaidens and servants are

37 Giustino Menescardi,
Abigail's Offer,
1749-53
oil on canvas, 205 x 365 cm.

behind Abigail, bearing gifts in wicker baskets and leading sheep and an ass. The episode symbolises the Virgin preventing the wrath of God from falling upon a sinful humanity.

38 Gaetano Zompini, *Rebekah at the Well*, 1749.

The youthful Rebekah is depicted at the well as she offers water to Eliezer, Abraham's steward, and his retinue of men and animals.

It was Eliezer who chose Rebekah to be Isaac's wife.

After a long period of infertility, the marriage produced Esau and the favoured son, Jacob. The scene is emblematic of the bounteous Virgin who succours sinners as well as the just.

39 **Giustino Menescardi**, *The Martyrdom of the Maccabees Before their Mother*, 1749-1753.

The Maccabees were the members of the Judaean dynasty of the Hasmoneans, who succeeded in driving the Seleucids from Syria form their land and re-instating the worship of Yahweh. The mother watches her seven sons being killed like Virgin watching the martyrdom of Christ on the Cross.

40 **Gaetano Zompini**, *Esther Faints Before Ahasuerus*, 1749.

Esther, a young Jewish woman, intercedes with the Persian king, Ahasuerus, to prevent the massacre of the

40 Gaetano Zompini,
Esther Faints Before Ahasuerus,
1749-53
oil on canvas, 205 x 520 cm.

people of Israel ordered by Haman, the chief minister of the Persians, among whom the Jews were living at the time. No one could go enter the king's presence without permission, on pain of death. Courageously risking her life, Esther appeared before Ahasuerus to plead her people's cause. Impressed by Esther's daring, the king agreed to listen to her and at that point, she fainted from excitement. The scene is symbolic of the Virgin's protection of the poor.

41 Giambattista Piazzetta, *Judith and Holophernes.*
Piazzetta here treats one of his favourite subjects in a nocturnal setting. Judith emerges from behind a curtain into a harsh beam of light that also falls across the drunken body of Holophernes, asleep on the bed. Her trepidation at the idea of killing him is clear from her expression, as she advances to cut his head off with the sword she carries in her left hand. In the shadow, we see the face of an old serving woman, observing proceedings with a diabolical satisfaction. In Zompini's iconographic scheme, the episode symbolises the defeat of hell, thanks to the Virgin's intervention. It appears that the painting was donated to the Scuola and placed in this space on the wall only after 1748.

38 Gaetano Zompini,
Rebekah at the Well,
1749-53
oil on canvas, 205 x 360 cm.

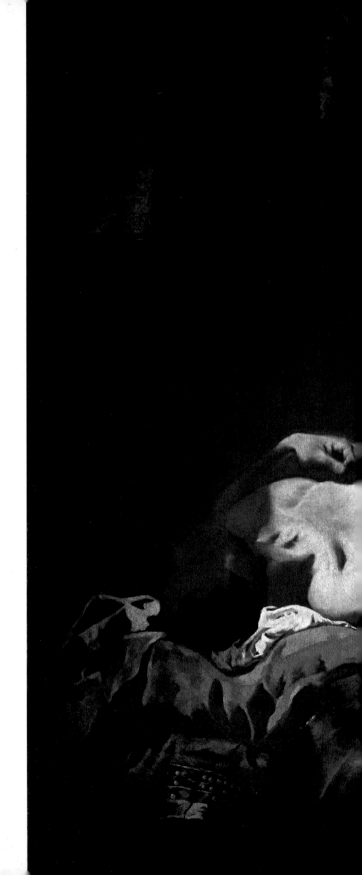

41 Giambattista Piazzetta,
Judith and Holophernes,
oil on canvas, 200 x 193 cm.

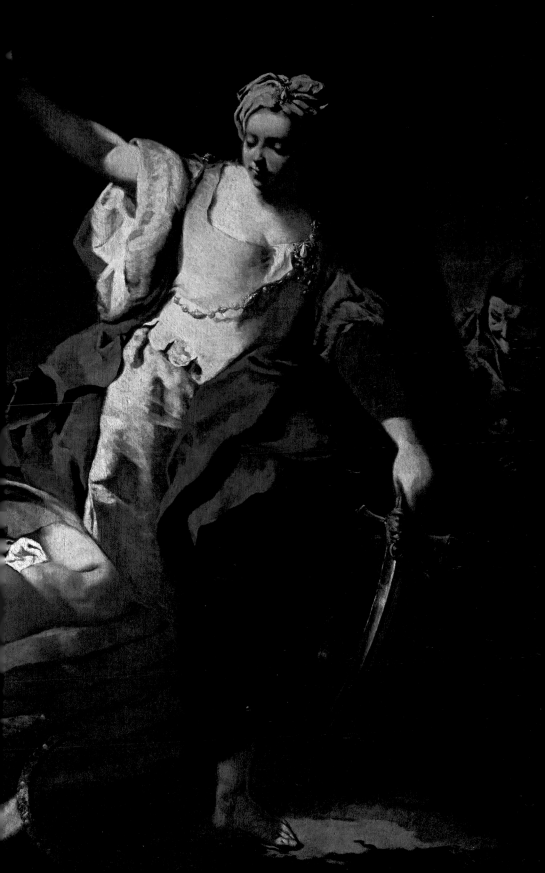

Sala dell'Albergo

The Sala dell'Albergo – *albergo* means "shelter" – is so called because it was originally intended as a reception room for poor, devout Brothers from Venice who venerated the Virgin, and before that to offer accommodation to pilgrims passing through the city on their way to the Holy Land. Later, the hall became the venue for meetings of the chancellery, chaired by the Guardian Grande.

The door leading to the Sala Capitolare is exactly the same as the one to the Sala dell'Archivio. Here, too, the top of the triangular tympanum reaches the corbelled frieze, the only surviving feature of an earlier seventeenth-century ceiling.

When Tiepolo was working in the Sala Capitolare, Padovanino's great painting was moved into the Sala dell'Albergo. This provided an opportunity to demolish the previous structure and replace it, after 1740, with the one we see today.

As in the previous hall, the ceiling here has been left in unfinished wood. The colouring and gilding that the original design certainly included were never carried out. Around the great central canvas of the Assumption is a series of oval compartments where the Prophets and Evangelists look down from slender, shallow, eighteenth-century frames.

The seventeenth-century walnut bench panels have an architectural design featuring doors with segmantal-arch tympana. These are marked off by two half-columns topped by capitals and surmounted by a corbel table. In the narrow space between the half-columns is the only concession to decoration, a festoon held at the top by the head of a putto. The floor is similar to that in the Sala dell'Archivio. It was designed and laid by the same craftsmen in the same period.

Following pages:
The Sala dell'Albergo and its floor inlaid with coloured marble.

The four colours of the marble alternate to form multiple stars inside oval or circular shapes framed by curved or straight strips.

Ceiling of the Sala dell'Albergo.

Ceiling

42 Alessandro Varotari known as Il Padovanino, *The Assumption of the Virgin*, 1634–38.

This huge painting was set in the centre of the Sala Capitolare ceiling in 1640, but was moved when Tiepolo was commissioned to complete the room's decoration in 1739. Padovanino had finished his work a century earlier, probably after 1634, when the plague in Venice was over, and before 1638, the year the Scuola was inaugurated.

The Virgin is seated on a throne of clouds, surrounded by winged putti and musician angels set around the edges of the painting. This leaves the centre section free for the backdrop of the heavens.

42 Alessandro Varotari known as
Il Padovanino,
The Assumption of the Virgin,
1634-38,
oil on canvas, 365 x 555 cm.

43 Giustino Menescardi,
Saint Luke with Bull,
1749-53
oil on canvas, 155 x 115 cm.

On the far side from the Virgin is an old bearded man carrying an olive branch in his hand. He is the prophet Elijah, the Biblical forerunner of the Carmelite order. At the mid point of the four sides, horizontal ovals portray the Evangelists, each which his traditional symbol, while at the corners are portraits of the great prophets associated with the theological privileges of the Virgin, 1749-1753.

Giustino Menescardi:

43 *Saint Luke with Bull,*

44 *Isaiah,*

45 *Saint Matthew with Angel*

46 *Jeremiah,*

47 *Saint John with Eagle*

48 *David*

49 *Saint Mark with Lion*

50 *Ezekiel.*

46 Giustino Menescardi,
Jeremiah,
1749-53
oil on canvas, 255 x 115 cm.

47 Giustino Menescardi,
Saint John with Eagle,
1749-53
oil on canvas, 155 x 115 cm.

52 Ambrogio Bon,
Adoration of the Shepherds,
1697,
oil on canvas, 205 x 535 cm.

Walls

In all likelihood, the paintings on the walls also date
from the early eighteenth century, and were thus the final stage in the decoration of the Sala dell'Albergo.
Some of these paintings have remained anonymous, as
it has not been possible to trace their authorship from
documentary records.

51 Anonymous, *The Virgin Appears to Saint Albert of Jeru-*
salem, (early eighteenth century)
Saint Albert was one of the Carmelite order's most venerated saints. His symbol was the lily an angel is offering him in the painting. The Virgin is on hand, holding
out the Carmelite habit. The volume on the ground is
probably the text of Albert's rule. In the neighbouring
church, an altar is dedicated to the saint, who is curing
the sick. Water brought into contact with the relics of
Saint Albert acquired miraculous powers.

52 Ambrogio Bon, *Adoration of the Shepherds*, 1697.

This work was donated by the Bancali, the Scuola's councillors, on 8 April 1697 and completed by Ambrogio Bon. He was a pupil of Johann Karl Loth, to whom the canvas was attributed until Moretti's correction. The scene is divided into two sections. On the left is the main group with the Virgin holding the Child up to God the Father, who reaches down from the clouds.

Saint Joseph kneels, with angels behind him. On the right is a group of shepherds, with sheep and oxen, and the scene is closed by a beturbaned boy bearing a large engraved metal vase.

The light spreading across the whole picture shines from the Holy Child. A warm, pinkish overall tonality was obtained by the use of reds and browns that are denser in the background, from which moving figures are emerging.

53 Antonio Balestra,
Joseph's Dream,
detail, 1703
oil on canvas, 205 x 240 cm.

53 **Antonio Balestra**, *Joseph's Dream*, 1703.

Joseph's body is relaxed in sleep as a winged angel draws near. Despite the painting's small dimensions, the artist has achieved a sober equilibrium and an intense interplay of light and shade throwing the two main figures into relief.

54 **Antonio Balestra**, *Rest on the Flight into Egypt*, 1703.

The painting extends horizontally to cover the entire wall, from the corner to the main entrance of the room. The group of the Virgin and Child with Saint Joseph is on the left of the painting. They are marked out by a light that spills over into the other areas, enlivened by the many angels and putti borne on the dark clouds in the sky. Note the deft compositional skills and the intense use of colour that critics ascribe to the Verona-born artist's contacts with the academic school at Rome.

55 **Anonymous**, *Virgin of Carmel*, early eighteenth century. The Virgin is depicted holding a number of scapulars. It has been conjectured that this painting was part of a larger work by Sante Piatti, who was called in between 1728 and 1733 by the Scuola, not just as an artist but also as a restorer.

56 **Anonymous**, *Venice in Ducal Attire Before the Virgin*, early eighteenth century. On the right of the picture, Venice, in the costume of the doge, kneels before the Virgin at the head of the thronging faithful. The Virgin is holding the scapular in one hand and, with the other, offers the Carmelite rule to Saint Simon Stock. A colonnade lends depth to the picture against a backdrop of mountains.

57 **Anonymous**, *The Presentation of Christ at the Temple*, early eighteenth century. The painting belongs to the series of episodes from the life of the Holy Child. The depiction of the Virgin reveals the immediacy of an artist – perhaps Trevisan – who has seen Tiepolo at first hand. The other female figure is the prophetess Anna with the Torah, the book of the Jewish law.

The façade of the Carmini church.

The Carmini church

The general plan reflected the one shared by all monastery churches of the so-called mendicant orders, for whom poverty and simplicity were outward signs of devotion. The surviving elements of that building are the exonarthex of the side entrance and the small brick arches in the aisle. Inside, it is laid out as a basilica, with a nave and two aisles, Istria stone columns and upturned basket capitals in the early Gothic idiom.

There are reports that the church was reconsecrated in 1348, probably after major structural work.

Further large-scale restructuring began in 1507, together with important decorative initiatives. Work continued in subsequent periods and the church's original appearance was radically altered as a result. The three structural changes were the construction of a new presbytery, with three polygonal apse chapels, the raising of the entire nave and part of the aisles to accommodate the large three-light, semicircular windows that make the interior so well-lit, and the transformation of the façade, which lost its original Gothic three-part ridge shape to take on a Renaissance appearance, with the semicircular central gable at the top and quarter-circle coping at the sides.

The apse chapels were added to the new transept area, extended by the presbytery at the nave. All are Renaissance constructions, with several orders of pillars on which the transept's great round arches rest. The organ and the friars' singing galleries face each other across the transept.

Despite a lack of written evidence, building work has been ascribed to Giovanni di Antonio Buora, an architect and sculptor from Lugano and follower of Pietro Lombardo. Buora was active at Venice until his death in 1513.

2 Lorenzo Lotto,
Saint Nicholas and Angels,
1529,
oil on canvas

As well as the church, the monastery was also renovated. A large round-arch cloister was built and the original decaying fourteenth-century bell tower was replaced by a tall campanile. It was erected in 1676 by Giuseppe Sardi, who died shortly afterwards and was buried in the church. The part of the church over the Gothic capitals comprises a huge wood and painted complex with statues of Biblical figures and saints linked to the Carmelite tradition, as well as a cycle of paintings illustrating the history of the order. Although begun in the sixteenth century, work on the cycle continued until the eighteenth. Artists involved included Andrea Celeste, Sebastiano Mazzoni and Pietro Liberi in the last decades of the seventeenth century and Gasparo Diziani, Girolamo Brusaferro and Giustino Menescardi in the 1740s.

The altars were also rebuilt in the seventeenth century and adorned with superb altarpieces like **1** *The Adoration of the Magi* by Cima da Conegliano (1509); **2** *Saint Nicholas and Angels* by Lorenzo Lotto (1529), commissioned by the fishmongers' Scuola; and **3**

The Presentation of Christ at the Temple by Jacopo Tintoretto (1543).

The central apse, its high altar erected in 1633, offers splendid wooden  stalls decorated with bas-relief heads of saints devoted to the Virgin of Carmel. They were carved by the Friulian Antonio Raffaelli (1668).

3 Jacopo Tintoretto,
*The Presentation of Jesus
at the Temple,*
1543,
oil on canvas

9 Girolamo Campagna,
*Candle-bearing angel
on the balustrade of the altar
at the Scuola,* 1617-18.

The altar of the Scuola in the Carmini church

The third altar in the righthand aisle belonged to the Scuola. It was granted to the Brothers in 1594 by the Carmelite friars, along with the area in front of it corresponding to several intercolumns.

The previous altar, dedicated to the Visitation, may have belonged to the women's association that made scapulars, and was torn down. The new Confraternity erected a different and more sumptuous altar in 1595. It was consecrated and given the new name of the "Altar of the Habit of the Virgin of Carmel". The notarised deed signed by the Brothers and the Carmelites for the reconstruction of the altar is dated 3 March 1595, and was drafted by the notary Francesco Mondo.

The altarpiece was completed and donated by the artist Pace Pace, a member of the Scuola, who was active between 1593 and 1617. Pace belonged to the group of friends and colleagues of Benedetto and Gabriele Caliari, respectively the brother and nephew of Paolo Veronese.

Pace's painting depicts the **5** *Virgin Bestowing the Scapular on Saint Simon Stock*. The scene is lent interest by the Brothers and saints present, Pope John XXII, Queen Blanca of Castile, Saint Louis king of France and another two lay figures who may be the Guardian Grande and Vicario of the day. John XXII is portrayed because he was the author of the Bolla Sabbatina, which sanctioned special privileges for believers who wore the scapular. The two Sisters present may indicate that women were admitted to the Scuola. We know from surviving records that the new altar was made of wood and, when it began to show evident signs of decay, was rebuilt in marble a century later. The new altar was completed about 1722 by Pietro Zangrando, an artist and designer of stage equipment for private receptions, historical events and religious celebrations.

The renovated altar was enlarged and raised. Pace's altarpiece was also extended downwards with an additional section representing souls in Purgatory, painted by Giovanni Fontana (1666-1725).

Two splendid large statues were placed on either side of the altar in 1722 or 1723. The statue of **6** *Humility* on the right is by Pagnano-born Giuseppe Torretti and the one on the left, representing **7** *Virginity*, is by Antonio Corradini, from Este.

These two artists also supplied putti and angel's heads for the altar. Sadly, the works were lost or destroyed during the nineteenth century, as were the bronze statuettes of the four Evangelists that adorned the tabernacle, designed by Giovanni Scalfarotto, who also designed the church of San Simeon Piccolo on the Grand Canal (1718-38).

In 1724, a double series of **8** wooden bench panels was affixed to the wall by the side of the altar. These were

10 Sebastiano Ricci, *Flight of Angels*, 1709

reserved for the Bancali, the members of the Chancellery. The wood carver commissioned was Francesco Bernardoni (1669-1730), a pupil of Giacomo Piazzetta and brother-in-law and partner of Giambattista Piazzetta. As Niero pointed out, there is a certain stylistic affinity between these carvings and the bench panels in the Sala dell'Archivio, which thus has a historical foundation as well as an artistic one.

The carvings focus on the *Five Miracles of the Virgin of Carmel*, an iconographic theme related to the cult of the Virgin, and at the same time to the Carmelite order itself. Reading from left to right, we see: the Virgin succouring a believer who has fallen from his horse into a well; the Virgin freeing a poor woman from demonic nocturnal temptations; the Virgin appearing to a poor cripple during a procession at Naples; the Virgin liberating a knight from slavery; and finally the Virgin putting out a fire at a bakery in Salerno.

The ceremonial space in front of the altar is closed off by a marble balustrade. At the two corners, there are two lovely kneeling **9** angels bearing candles, executed in bronze by Girolamo Campagna in 1617-18. Above the altar and the roof of the aisle, a new space was created to form a double vault and lateral three-light semicircular windows that allows more light into the structure beneath.

Pietro Bianchini was called in to complete the stuccoes, probably to drawings by Abbondio Stazio. In 1709, Sebastiano Ricci frescoed the new vault with a breathtakingly **10** elegant flight of angels, whose impact derives from the gilded surface of a light-filled sky in which angels soar, bringing divine blessings.

Index of names

Bibliography

Boschini M., *Le ricche minere della pittura veneziana, (The Rich Mines of Venetian Painting)*, Venice 1674.

Caravia A., *Il sogno di Caravia, (Caravia's Dream)*, Venice 1541.

Comoli G., *Cenni storici sull'origine della Confraternita e Scuola dei Carmini in Venezia, (Historical Notes on the Origin of the Confraternity and Scuola dei Carmini in Venice)*, Venice 1904.

Franzoi U., *Le Chiese di Venezia, (The Churches of Venice)*, Venice 1976.

Logan O., *Venezia cultura e società*, (originally published in English as *Culture and Society in Venice, 1470-1790. The Renaissance and its Heritage, London 1972*), Rome 1980.

Lorenzetti G., *Venezia e il suo estuario, (Venice and Her Estuary)*, Rome 1963.

Mariacher G., *Mostra delle tre Scuole, (Exhibition of the Three Schools)*, Venice1947.

Mariuz A., *L'opera completa del Piazzetta, (The Complete Works of Piazzetta)*, Milan, 1982.

Moretti L., *Antonio Molinari rivisitato, (Antonio Molinari Re-assessed)*, in "Arte Veneta", XXXIII (1979), pp. 59–69.

Moretti L., *Santo Piatti*, in "Arte Veneta", XL (1986), pp. 128–139.

Moretti L. – Branca Savini S., *Chiesa di Santa Maria de Carmini. Arte e devozione, (The Church of Santa Maria dei Carmini. Art and Devotion)*, Venice 1995.

Niero A., *Scuola Grande dei Carmini*, Venice 1991.

Perotti L., *Memorie sui luoghi pii, (Memorials on Holy Sites)*, Venice 1991.

Pignatti T. – Pedrocco F., *Giambattista Tiepolo. Itinerari veneziani, (Giambattista Tiepolo. Venetian Itineraries)*, Venice 1996.

Pignatti T. – Pullan B., *Le Scuole di Venezia, (The Scuole of Venice)*, Milan 1981.

Pullan B., *La politica sociale della Repubblica di Venezia, 1500–1620, (The Social Policy of the Republic of Venice. 1500-1620)*, Rome 1982.

Ruggeri U., *Alessandro Varotari, detto il Padovanino, (Alessandro Varotari, known as Il Padovanino)*, in "Saggi e memorie di Storia dell'Arte", 1988, pp. 101 ss.

Semenzato G., *L'architettura di Baldassare Longhena, (The Architecture of Baldassare Longhena)*, Padua 1954.

Sansovino F., *Venezia città nobilissima et singolare, (Venice Most Noble and Singular City)*, Venice 1581.

Scarfi S., *L'attività pittorica di Gaetano Zompini, (The Painting Career of Gaetano Zompini)*, in "Venezia Arti", 1994, pp. 77–84.

Stringa G., *Venezia città nobilissima et singolare et ora con molta diligenza corretta..., (Venice Most Noble and Singular City and Now with Great Diligence Corrected ...)*, Venice 1604.

Zanetti A. M., *Descrizione di tutte le pubbliche pitture della città di Venezia, (Description of All the Public Paintings of the City of Venice)*, Venice 1733.

Documents in the Archivio di Stato at Venice

Consiglio dei Dieci (Council of Ten) – Parti Comuni (General Deliberations) Envelope No. 1136 Decree 27 April 1767.

Scuola Grande dei Carmini – Capitolare 2°, c. 159, 161, 164, 169.

Printed at Grafiche Vianello
Ponzano/Treviso/Italy
in the month of September 2003